Self-motivation

Self-motivation

Gael Lindenfield

Illustrations by Jessica Stockham

Thorsons
An Imprint of HarperCollins*Publishers*

To Jane Graham-Maw, my editor,
with love and much gratitude for
so sensitively underpinning my own
self-motivation for the last five years.

Thorsons
An Imprint of HarperCollins*Publishers*
77–85 Fulham Palace Road,
Hammersmith, London W6 8JB
1160 Battery Street,
San Francisco, California 94111–1213

Published by Thorsons 1996
10 9 8 7 6 5 4 3

© Gael Lindenfield 1996

Gael Lindenfield asserts the moral right to
be identified as the author of this work

A catalogue record for this book
is available from the British Library

ISBN 0 7225 3244 X

Printed in Great Britain by
Caledonian International Book Manufacturing, Glasgow

Contents

Acknowledgements

In relation to this book, it is to my husband Stuart that I am most grateful. Even though his own working life is now so very absorbing and busy, he has never failed to give me emotional support and practical help when the demands of writing have taken their toll on my mental and physical energy. As usual he has also acted as amateur in-house editor, correcting, on demand, my dyslexic and ungrammatical text.

As usual I am also grateful to my clients, who have experimented with many of the ideas and techniques which this book contains.

I'd also like to thank the many friends who provided me with their Quick-fixes, and those who have given me quotes, poems and book references. In particular I'd like to thank Chrissie Castagnetti for introducing me to 'Brain Gym' exercises and literature.

Finally, my gratitude and admiration goes out again to Jessica Stockham, who always astounds me with her ability to translate my 'wishy-washy' ideas for illustrations into such meaningful and amusing drawings.

Introduction

A serious new energy crisis is gathering force. But the depleting power of this one is different. It doesn't fuel factories, cars, cookers or computers. It drives humans.

The resource that is diminishing at an alarming rate is human motivation.

To prove my point, I cannot quote you any meaningful statistics and figures. But do I need to? The compelling evidence is all around us. If you just look around at the people you meet in your everyday life and those whom you know less directly through the media, you can see and hear for yourself the obvious 'tell-tale' signs...Perhaps you are even feeling some of these symptoms of dwindling reserves of motivation within yourself:

- **Apathy**
  - *'I can't be bothered anymore...I'll just let them get on with it.'*
  - *'How am I? Oh, same as usual – surviving.'*
  - *'I wouldn't waste my energy on them.'*
  - *'...anyway, if I had more money I'd only spend it, so there's no point in pushing myself.'*
  - *'Success doesn't bring you happiness – you might just as well stick with what you've got and be thankful for small mercies.'*
- **Insensitivity**
  - *'I'm past caring now – so what if I do get fat or die five years early?'*
  - *'You see so much suffering around, you get immune to it. There's no point in getting upset.'*
  - *'I used to feel guilty and want to do something, but now I think I've got enough to do looking after my own.'*

- 'They *don't care or do anything, so why should I? Nobody thanks you if you try anyway.'*
- **Powerlessness**
  - 'What's the point of fighting for more?…They'll do it whatever.'
  - 'You're at their mercy nowadays – what we want counts for nothing.'
  - 'You're just a pawn for their profit – they've got the power. Your happiness and health are not important.'
  - 'You can't afford to stand up for yourself these days. You're branded as a troublemaker. I need this job even if I am being ripped off.'
  - 'I might as well let destiny take its course. Who am I to fight it?'
- **Escapism**
  - 'Why not enjoy yourself while you can? – Double whisky, please.'
  - 'I don't think about it – I'd go mad or "top myself" if I did.'
  - 'What's wrong with legalizing cannabis and Ecstasy? – With the way the world's going, we need them and probably more.'
  - 'I just live from day to day and hope I win the lottery.'

So do we need to wait for a research project or Government report to prove conclusively how damaging the loss of the psychological power of self-motivation is? It is obvious that it isn't just individuals who suffer in the long term. The future of the earth and humanity are threatened as well.

I am well aware that this is not the whole picture and that there are still many positive, inspired people around. But negativity is very contagious, and with our global mass media it can spread alarmingly quickly. Good news, we are told, doesn't sell papers or attract viewers. So, as the countdown to the new millennium reaches its last lap, we are constantly being fed with demotivating prophesies and promises of self-destructive trends. For example, we are told that we can look forward to:

– even less job security, with organizations continuing to get leaner and robots and computers becoming more and more sophisticated

– even less comfort and support as our families and communities continue to disintegrate

– worse health, as pollution increases and the earth's natural resources become even more depleted

– more violence as our population explodes and the Third World and other disadvantaged groups learn how to fight more aggressively for their fair share

Having spent too much of my early life feeling and behaving like a helpless victim, I was determined not to let this kind of crystal-ball gazing get to me. I therefore took myself to my 'thinking hole' in Spain and pondered the problem until I came up with a positive practical response. This book is it!

Why I Chose to Write a Book on *Self*-motivation

1   It is the only kind of motivation which I believe we can rely on to carry us on into the new world.

Traditional 'carrots' in the form of money, promotion, medals and fame are no longer dependable. There are now too many of us fighting for too few chances. No one needs to seduce us into achieving. If we do not reach the target or required standard (either at work or at home) we can be simply and mercilessly replaced.

2   It is the kind of motivation which I know most about.

Being brought up by an alcoholic mother and in inadequately staffed children's homes, I learned about the power of self-motivation at an early age. In order merely to survive and achieve success of any description, I had to find the drive from within myself. I quickly learned that no one else cared that much about me or my potential. In fact, my reality was that the more I succeeded the less attention and other rewards I was given. I was seen to be the one who could look after herself, and was lucky enough to be bright and capable enough to get by on my own without much encouragement or incentives.

These prematurely forced seeds of my own self-motivation are therefore deeply rooted. They were further strengthened by an adulthood which gave them plenty of opportunity to flourish. Not surprisingly with my childhood history, I have had many personal setbacks with which to contend such as severe depression, career mistakes and a divorce.

But my knowledge on the subject is not all personal. The pattern of my working life has been one which has enabled my self-motivation to gather strength and skills. Throughout my career as a therapist, I have been constantly engaged in starting up difficult pioneering projects in a 'Cinderella' field of mental health. More recently as a trainer in the new, challenging world of business, I have acquired considerable knowledge and expertise which has enabled me to help professionals at all levels to maintain a high degree of self-motivation.

Finally, I have had a period of unemployment and many years' experience of self-employment to draw on. I have managed to keep my own motivation thriving throughout the ebbs and flows of success which my own consultancy business inevitably had to weather in our recent tough recession.

3   It is the Rolls Royce of motivation.

Self-motivation has more strength, power and durability than any other kind. Although it may take considerable time and energy to build, it is far superior in quality to any of the external incentives which are offered us as inducements.

4   I am inspired by challenges!

One of the characteristics of highly self-motivated people is they enjoy the excitement of venturing alone into uncharted territory. When I first saw that this subject was so important and relevant to current concerns, I researched the appropriate literature. I couldn't find any book which offered a) an analysis of the components of this vital psychological power and b) gave practical advice on how it can be built and boosted. From the moment I became aware of this glaring gap in the Personal Development bookshelves, I felt 'driven' to fill it!

You may be interested to know that the actual writing and completion of this book have proved to be the greatest tests of my own self-motivation. This past year of my life has included so many setbacks which were genuinely not of my own making that I've begun to wonder if gremlins really do exist! But even if they do, I now know that their sabotage will never get the better of my self-motivation!

Who Can Be Helped by This Book?

Anyone and everyone who is:

- *fed up with kicking and shouting at themselves* to 'get on with it' and is looking for a more positive and effective motivational strategy
- considering *self-employment*, but is afraid that their willpower may let them down (or those who are self-employed and find their willpower *is* letting them down!)
- *applying for a job* which specifies 'a high degree of self-motivation' as an essential requirement (and what job advert doesn't make this demand nowadays?!)
- consistently *giving up on highly desired self-set personal goals* such as dieting, giving up smoking, learning a language or simply keeping the house tidy and well-maintained
- is aware that they are *playing too safe with their life* and is looking for an extra way of boosting their determination to make some radical changes
- keen to *help other people become more self-motivated* and has tried every other 'trick in the book' to get them moving into action by themselves

What This Book Offers

A complete self-help programme to help you develop aspects of your personality which will enable you to become consistently self-motivated and help others to do the same.

Section 1:

Introduces **36 personality characteristics** which I believe are the inner 'Drivers' of people who are successful self-motivators. Each of these 36 areas is divided into three parts:

1 explanation of the nature of the Driver and why it is relevant to self-motivation
2 practical tips on how these Drivers can be built and boosted
3 an Instant Exercise to give you a chance immediately to test and develop your psychological strength in this area.

Section 2:

A selection of **'Quick-fix' techniques** collected from a number of people whom I know to be highly self-motivated. You will find many ideas on how to give your own motivation a boost after a setback.

Section 3:

How to build **self-motivation in others**, using the two roles of Leader and Parent as examples.

Section 4:

Further Help. This includes a **selection of books and cassettes** which I and people with whom I have worked have found useful. Many of the quotations used throughout the book are taken from authors in this list.

Section 5:

Your **Notebook**: Headed blank pages for you to use for your own thoughts as you read through, and also to help you work through the Instant Exercises.

Index

For quick reference to any other parts of the book to which you might want to refer.

How to Use This Book as a Self-help Programme

Those of you who have read my previous books will find the style of this one different. In planning it, I was aware that people who are interested in self-motivation are usually very busy, with little time to plough through long texts. I have therefore chosen to organize this book into brief self-contained parts which can easily be read and worked on in short periods of time (approximately 30 – 60 minutes).

Whether you are working on your own or as part of a small group, I would suggest that to get the best from this book you should follow this sequence:

1 *Read the book section by section*, making notes in the relevant blank pages provided at the back of the book. The Instant Exercises are included to help you test your strength in each area, so don't skip these at this stage.
2 Take approximately *one hour of time to review your notes* and decide which of the sections are most appropriate to your needs. List these in some order of priority.
3 *Make an action plan (see page 234)* for doing some personal development work in the areas you wish to improve. Use the tips in each section to help you set specific timed goals – but remember, don't give yourself too much to do too quickly!

4 Leave the book in a handy place so that it can also be used as a *reference guide*, especially during periods when you know you will need an extra boost of self-motivation. Key words in the introductions to the Drivers and all the tips have been highlighted so that you can use these as a quick checklist.

I hope this programme sounds exciting to you. I have enjoyed creating it.

If it should begin to feel too much like hard work and you are doubting your ability to stick with it, *please* continue to read on. This is the book for YOU!

The 36 Secrets of Successful Self-motivation

*A self-help programme designed to help
build and boost the specific personality
characteristics which drive self-motivation*

In this section we will explore the 36 personality characteristics which I have identified as being crucial to long-lasting self-motivation. Some people who have been lucky with their genetic inheritance, parenting and schooling have these firmly rooted in their adult psychological selves. Self-motivation therefore appears to come 'naturally' to them. The majority of us, however, are less fortunate. But we no longer have to sigh and wish we were 'made' differently. We can now choose to develop these characteristics. This section, therefore, not only explains what these characteristics are about, it also offers tips on how to develop them and exercises which will help you get started instantly.

Please note that these 36 'Personality Drivers' are not listed in order of their importance, nor is the length of text they have been allocated an indication of their value. Some are shorter than others because I have written at great length on the subject before or because I consider other authors (*listed in Section 4*) to have more expertise in that particular area.

If ever you begin to feel daunted by the amount of personal development work you want to do, remind yourself that best results are achieved by taking a step-by-step approach and making sure that there are always plenty of rewards and fun *en route*.

Driver 1

Visionary Thinking
– without Idle Dreaming

(Notebook page 216)

Vision is the art of seeing things invisible.

JONATHAN SWIFT

 'Amazing – so you are actually now living your dream!' I'll never forget these words. They were said to me a number of years ago by a friend whom I had not seen for five years. They had such an emotional impact on me that every minute detail of our chance meeting is imprinted on my memory.

My friend was totally right. I was living my dream, but I was so thoroughly enjoying doing so and involved in planning its realization that I hadn't appreciated the extent of my success!

The reason my friend knew so much about my life-dream was that, a few years previously, we had been students together on a Dramatherapy course. During one of our training sessions the group had helped me enact some of my 'idle fantasies', and I participated in a dramatization of a scene which, with hindsight, now seems to have been eerily prophetic.

With the help of the group, for approximately half an hour I simply played (just as children do) at being the person I wanted to be, with the lifestyle I wanted to have. I showed people around my beautiful house in the sun and talked about the courses I was leading there and the book I had just written. I introduced friends to my new partner and we played out an easy comfortable scene in our role as co-parents to my two daughters.

Prior to this time, even though the rational thinker in me knew that I could probably make each aspect of my 'dream' come true, I had taken virtually no action towards making any of them likely to happen.

The exercise was not an easy one for me, particularly at the time. I was still deeply emotionally (and financially!) bruised from my recent divorce. I was living alone with my two young daughters and my daily life was undoubtedly focused on short-term subsistence goals. I was working part-time at a job which was innovative and rewarding but also exceedingly low paid and exhausting.

During times of loneliness at home I would dream of a potential new partner with whom to share my life and children. During times of stress at work I dreamed of finding a quiet place in the sun where I could run my courses and perhaps write the book which I knew my clients needed.

Why did such a simple fun exercise have such an impact on my motivation?

First, it helped me to *feel* some of the pleasure and enjoyment which the realization of my dreams would bring. Research shows that *we are much more likely to achieve goals which trigger off strong emotions in us*.

Secondly, the exercise implanted an unforgettable *inspiring, vivid image* in my subconscious. Even imaginary seeing is believing! My daydreaming was no longer a jumble of meandering unconnected images which left me feeling wistful and wishful. My new visions were lifelike, linked and consistent – more like a believable documentary than a whimsical fairy-story. Research has also proved that *the more belief we have in our goals, the more likely they are to be achieved*. It's no wonder that, recently, many of the biggest best-sellers in the management book world are about how to form and communicate a company's vision.

> *I saw in my mind hundreds of McDonalds restaurants in all the corners of the land.*
>
> RAY CROC

> *Projecting your mind into a successful situation is the most powerful means to achieve goals. If you spend time with pictures of failure in your mind, you will orchestrate failure.*
>
> ESTÉE LAUDER

There is yet another interesting (and hopefully useful) aspect to my personal story which illustrates how we can sometimes use our visionary thinking from the past to help us motivate ourselves in the present. It concerns my reasons for joining the Dramatherapy course in the first place.

The breakdown of my first marriage did for me what it does for most people: It spurred me into introspection and forced me to ponder on all the other regrets of my life. Fortunately, the wisdom I had gained from surviving many previous life-crises assured me that although my heart was at that time twisted with scorn and despair, I could use my head to make something positive out of this crisis.

As a result, I consciously took time to out to re-visit and re-appraise some *long-lost dreams*. In doing so I recalled that as a teenager I had a very clear vision of the ideal job for me – a director of documentary drama. Re-kindling this childish fantasy helped me see that, at heart, I was still a girl who thrived on drama and had a burning mission to right injustice in the world!

Once I had brought myself back down to my mundane earth of an over-sized mortgage and three mouths to feed, I accepted yet again that documentary drama was an unachievable career goal for me. But, the difference this time was that I did allow myself to look for *an acceptable compromise.* In my search for one I found the Dramatherapy course and my new inspiring dream.

But (in case you were beginning to wonder!) painful divorces and Dramatherapy training are not the only routes to productive visionary thinking. Fortunately, there are many other ways of consciously and proactively stimulating this aspect of our potential! Below I am listing a few possibilities. As you read them tick the ones which interest you and note down any new ones you may think of yourself.

The soul never thinks without a picture.

ARISTOTLE

 # Tips: Visionary Thinking – without Idle Dreaming

❑ Set aside specific periods of relaxed, *uninterrupted time* for daydreaming and gazing into your own personal crystal ball.

❑ Use the picture power of your imagination, or art or drama to fix a vivid, detailed, inspiring image of your *desired future* in your subconscious mind. (Remember, this part of our mind prefers simple pictures.)

❑ Strengthen the power of these images by choosing *pleasurable sounds and smells* to associate with your dream (for example, aromatherapy oils and uplifting music can help).

❑ Keep a *symbolic reminder* of your vision constantly within your conscious sight or hearing (a picture in your diary or on the fridge; a small object or piece of fabric, etc. to fit into a briefcase or make-up bag).

❑ Use an *enthusiastic, emotional tone* to talk frequently about your vision (but only to people who are interested and supportive).

❑ Read books and watch films about *'big-thinking' people* who have also had (and have acted on) vision.

❑ Arrange to *visit the location* (or a similar one) where your vision is set (e.g. a holiday; a trip to the estate agent; a snoop into the board room).

❑ Constantly check that your *daily action planning* and activities are on the same 'wavelength' as *your* vision of success (e.g. 'how does working overtime four nights a week fit with my vision of having found my ideal partner or making a memorable contribution to my community or living well to an advanced age?')

Instant Exercise: Visionary Thinking – without Idle Dreaming

1 Think of a goal you want to achieve in the future.
2 Close your eyes; take three slow deep breaths, and then for one or two minutes use your mind's eye to conjure up a picture of yourself having successfully achieved your goal.
3 Write down a resolution connected to this dream which is achievable within the next 24 hours – for example, 'I will ring the library on Tuesday for addresses of adventure holiday companies/colleges/dating agencies.'

You've got to think about 'big things' while you are doing small things, so that the small things go in the right direction.

ALVIN TOFFLER

Driver 2

Unashamed Neediness
– without Selfish Greediness

(Notebook page 216)

> *One must not lose desires. They are mighty stimulants to creativeness, to love and to a long life.*
> ALEXANDER BOGOMOLETZ

 Neediness is not an attribute that most people would first associate with self-motivated high achievers. In fact, in our society it is likely to be the last. Neediness and 'weediness' have, after all, become almost synonymous partners in the English language. Both are equally feared and despised. To confess to either is to risk both self-dislike and disdain from others.

This cultural prejudice against neediness often presents a big problem for people who are thirsting for more self-motivation. How I can empathize! I have failed to achieve many goals in my life simply because I tried to kid *myself* that I wasn't needy.

Although the language I used to talk to myself out of doing what I needed to do may not have been so embarrassingly explicit, the excuses were, in essence:

'It would be nice to be half a stone lighter, but *I* don't need to be thin to be loved.'

'I'd love to be paid well for my work, but I don't need money to be happy.'

'I could be a better organized person, but I don't need a tidy desk and an empty in-tray to feel in control.'

'I'd love to be better friends with...but I don't need any more close friends.'

With a little help from confrontative counselling, eventually I stopped pretending. It was a relief to own up to my neediness – I hadn't realized how much energy I was using to deny and conceal it.

The next step was even harder – I had to learn to view my neediness as a friend rather than a foe. It was a long time before I could see it as a potentially positive force which could help me, and others, have more of what we *wanted* in life. I now firmly believe not only that *motivated people are needy people, but that self-motivated people are even more needy people!*

It was comforting news for me while researching this book to find that almost every theory on motivation I came across confirmed this belief. Perhaps the most well known of these is that of the American psychologist Abraham Maslow, who arrived at his conclusions from studying the motivational patterns of a very wide range of successful people. Although some of Maslow's ideas are now considered a bit dated and limiting by many of today's motivation gurus, I still find the following insights he gave us very useful:

- Our needs tend to develop on an ascending scale ranging from basic physiological ones up to the more 'luxurious' ones such as self-fulfilment (*see illustration below*).
- Once we have satisfied one set of needs we tend to progress quite naturally on to the next set.
- We cannot be easily motivated by factors which are concerned with the needs in a category which is higher in the scale than where we are currently based (that is, it not very motivating to remind ourselves of the benefits a project can bring to our mind and soul, when our stomach is crying out for food or we are gripped by the terror of impending redundancy).
- We cannot be easily motivated by factors which are concerned with getting our lower needs met when we have moved further up the hierarchy (that is, highlighting the security payoffs of a deal is not very motivational to someone who is adequately fed and housed and is thirsting for adventure).

- The lower the need we are experiencing happens to be in the hierarchy, the stronger the urge will be to get it met (that is, we find it easier to motivate ourselves to do boring work which pays the mortgage than to join an evening class which we know will introduce us to some interesting new people).
- If our circumstances change, our motivational needs may also change (for example, when I become ill, I find myself more [but still not very!] attracted to routine household activities, because doing them gives me a feeling of stability and security).

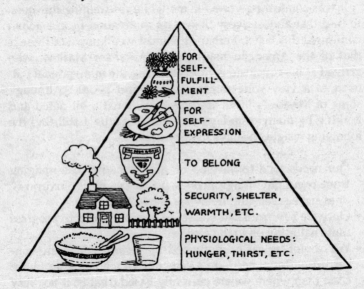

FOR SELF-FULFILLMENT

FOR SELF-EXPRESSION

TO BELONG

SECURITY, SHELTER, WARMTH, ETC.

PHYSIOLOGICAL NEEDS: HUNGER, THIRST, ETC.

Perhaps while reading this you have begun to think of examples from your own and others' experience which contradict these 'rules'. Theories about human behaviour always produce these problems, but the following tips, which I and others have found very useful, have been largely based on Maslow's ideas.

Tips: Unashamed Neediness – without Selfish Greediness

❑ Be *open and honest* to both yourself and others about your needs.
❑ Make sure that your basic survival needs are being adequately catered for before trying to motivate yourself to pursue 'higher' goals.
❑ If your motivation is sluggish for a particular project or task, *identify* which of your needs it may be able to help satisfy.
❑ Use motivational *self-talk* which is directly in line with this need (such as, 'I want to get this report written because I need to keep my job/have good self-esteem/be of service to the community').
❑ If you are still struggling to get your needs at the lower end of the scale met, but feel guilty about not pursuing goals at the higher end, *write down some goals* you would like to give yourself when you are ready (for example, 'When I have finished this course, I will set aside some time to do some voluntary work' or 'As soon as the last payment on the loan for the car is paid, I will make a contribution to Oxfam').

If possible, show these goals to a friend and then put them away in a file or envelope marked 'future projects'.
❑ If you are still equating getting *your* needs met with either 'weediness' or 'greediness', write the following *affirming statement* on a card and read it out loudly and regularly (particularly before going to sleep):
'I accept my neediness and it is in my control.'

Instant Exercise: Unashamed Neediness – without Selfish Greediness

1 Look at the illustration of Maslow's hierarchy and, in relation to your most pressing current needs (e.g. more money/love/personal power, etc.), mark where you would place yourself.
2 Put an age marker at the side of each band to mark the time when you plan to put the other needs at the top of your priority list (e.g. Self-fulfilment – 85!)
3 Identify two *specific* pressing needs you want to keep top of your priority list for the next month. Share these with a friend and/or pin up a reminder in a prominent place:

This month's priority **NEEDS** are:
A to clear my pending tray
B to lose half a kilo

Let us train our minds to desire what the situation demands.
                                                              SENECA

Driver 3

Eternal Optimism – without Denying Common Sense

(Notebook page 217)

The world belongs to optimists, pessimists are only spectators.
FRANÇOIS GUIZOT

 For at least 20 years of my adult life I firmly believed that optimism and 'common sense' were totally incompatible. I viewed the world as a dangerous, disappointing place inhabited by dangerous, disappointing people. But I certainly did not see this outlook as a handicap – quite the contrary. I was proud to be a pessimist – it was a sign that I was not just intelligent but also sane.

As a 'realist' (the label I preferred to give myself), I felt safer and more in control. Because I expected the worst, I had the firm illusion that I could avoid many setbacks, disasters and hurts. The fact that I continually experienced more than my 'fair share' of the latter did nothing to shift my belief – it merely confirmed it. It proved to me that not only was life guaranteed to let you down, it was guaranteed to let some people (including me) down more than others.

Needless to say, this outlook had a considerable impact on my self-motivation. The only goals that could have real inspiring appeal for me were those that offered immediate and obvious rewards. I saw little point in wasting energy on trying for anything else – only the totally mad or totally stupid could be motivated to set themselves challenging, long-term goals. My 'superior' friends were the first to agree that you have to be daft, for example, to kick yourself into:

- working for exams you may never need
- saving for a pension that you'd be too old to spend
- improving relationships which were pre-destined to fail
- keeping fit when you know you'll die!

With hindsight I can fully understand how I drifted into the work that I did. I became a social worker specializing in helping people with chronic and generally incurable problems. Needless to say, I did not meet many optimists in that area of my life either!

Now here I am promoting positive thinking for a living, and I am convinced that I am not daft, mad or even bad to do so!

I don't believe that a miracle has happened and I don't believe that I have been brainwashed. I believe that I have been converted by an incontestable mound of fact.

The conversion started when I began to act *as though I were an optimist*. For a variety of irrelevant reasons, I eventually found myself socializing and working among people who took the opposite view to me. It was obvious that not only were they enjoying life more than I was, but they were also much more successful in their work and personal relationships. In addition, they were more committed to making the long-term changes in the world which I so desperately wanted and needed to see. Being in this climate and also being in the world of therapy, I began to search out (contrary to my normal habit of disdainful dismissal) the new positive thinking literature and research which was beginning to fill the psychology bookshelves.

For several more years I experimented and tested these theories and techniques, not just on my own negative demons, but on hundreds more that I met through my work. I found that for hardened pessimists like myself and my clients, some of the approaches and advice were too simplistic or too implausible. (However long I talk to myself in the mirror, I doubt if I'll ever be convinced that I can achieve *anything* I set my mind to.)

I therefore set about devising my own strategies, and as

positive thinking began to impact not just on our moods but on our behaviour and relationships, my cynicism gradually faded. At some stage in the process, I became aware that *I was no longer* playing *at being an optimist, I actually* was *one!*

Of course in times of stress, I have felt myself slip back. It's hard (if not impossible) to undo half a life-time's conditioning. But when this happens, I know there are tried and tested strategies which I can use to lift me back into the world of motivated optimists.

The following tips will help keep you positively orientated, but if your pessimism is deeply rooted, additional time spent on 'correcting' your thinking by attending courses or counselling could only be a worthwhile investment. But choose your courses carefully, making sure that they do not dismiss the power of common sense.

> *The danger with a lot of positive thinking training is that some people can become unbearably and unrealistically positive – so heavenly that they are no earthly good.*
>
> RICHARD DENNY

Alternatively, you could work through some additional self-help programmes. Two of my own earlier books, *The Positive Woman* and *Self-esteem*, both have many positive thinking exercises and strategies and I have recommended several others in Section 4.

 ## Tips: Eternal Optimism – without Denying Common Sense

❏ Programme your subconscious to have a *positive image* of optimists by repeating over and over again affirming sentences such as:
'I enjoy being an optimist.'
'Optimism works and wins'.

'It's not cool to be cynical, it's crazy.'

❑ *Start and finish each day* with some positive and uplifting input into your mind (such as, by reading a good book, listening to music or watching 'upbeat' TV). Avoid reading, watching or listening to pessimistic or negative material at these crucial times when your subconscious mind is very impressionable.

❑ Use optimistic and positive (but still realistic) *language and sayings* to talk about whatever project you are trying to motivate yourself to do or finish (for example, 'the harder this is to finish the more satisfaction I will feel when it is done' or 'the sooner I have started the sooner I will have finished').

❑ *Ban pessimistic and cynical self-talk* and 'ain't it awful' conversations with friends, even the humorous kind, such as 'I'm a born loser – I don't know why you bother,' 'It would be just my luck, if after all this effort…' or 'Don't count your chickens…'

❑ Before starting on a difficult project, read an autobiography or watch a video about a *successful person*.

❑ Regularly dip into a book of *optimistic quotes* which you could keep handy on your desk or bedside table (*see Section 4 for suggestions*).

❑ Put up *pictures or photos* of optimistic friends or famous people (I kept a picture of Oprah Winfrey in my purse when I was trying to motivate myself to do more work with the media – and it worked!).

❑ Say a firm *'no' to spending time with pessimists* and negative talkers when you are trying to motivate yourself (– and why not tell them why you are avoiding them as well?!). If you find this difficult, use the tips in Driver 27 (*page 138*) to help you brush up your assertive skills.

❑ *Furnish* your office and home with uplifting pictures, colours and plants.

❑ Talk to young *happy children* about what they are doing and what plans they have for the future (their optimism is very infectious and may stimulate the cheerful child in you!).

Instant Exercise: Eternal Optimism – without Denying Common Sense

- Acknowledge (by speaking out loud if possible) three experiences, however simple and mundane, which you are looking forward to within the next week.
- Remind yourself of three good experiences which you have planned for yourself within the next year which you are confident you will enjoy (if they are not in your diary, plan and enter them *now*!).
- Write down three experiences in your life which turned out to be much better than even your common sense expected (a particular party/film/job/friendship).

Driver 4

Guru-worshipping
– without Blind Following

(Notebook page 217)

The really great make you feel that you too can become great.
MARK TWAIN

 When I recently saw *myself* described in a magazine as a 'Self-help Guru', my emotional system was instantly thrown into a state of uncomfortable confusion. One second it was sending me signals of pleasure and pride, and the next, fear and anxiety.

Of course the media like to label people, but even so this set me thinking. When I stopped to consider what I was feeling (and what I thought I ought to be feeling!), I realized that not only did I have mixed feelings about having reached a stage in my career where I had this status and its awesome responsibility, but I also had mixed feelings about gurus in general. In order to sort my emotional muddle out, I took several steps which I thought would be useful to share. They could be used as a self-enquiry route for anyone else who has mixed feelings about 'guru-power'.

Step One:

I searched in dictionaries to clarify the meaning of the word and then devised my own brief secular and neutral *definition* which is as follows:

A guru is an inspirational theoretician and leader of a movement.

Step Two:

I asked myself to think of the many *beneficial changes* through-out history which gurus have initiated and supported. I was surprised at how many examples I could think of.

Step Three:

I looked at my own personal history and *acknowledged the inspiration* I had drawn from people who, although less well known, had considerable guru-appeal for me. Perhaps I could have turned my life around without such people, but would I have wanted to? I know that even today when my motivation is flagging I can still give myself a buzz of pleasure and energy just by recalling their faces or words.

Step Four:

I reflected on the kind of gurus and followers which I had felt led to *negative outcomes* for both myself and others.

Step Five:

I reflected on the positive guru aspects of my *own leadership role*. I recalled the kind of feedback which I am continually receiving, even from people whom I have never met. Over and over again I am thanked not just for my professional skills and knowledge, but for being an inspirational role model.

Step Six:

I confronted myself with the occasions when I thought the 'guru factor' had *blocked the growth* of some of my clients' own personal power. It was usually when they had become *too* in awe of me or too dependent on me. I noted what we had done that had helped correct this situation.

These six self-reflective steps certainly helped me to sort out my emotional muddle and have clarified which aspects of guru-power are useful and which are not. It also helped to compile the following list of tips. But please remember that I am still definitely a novice in this field, so if any of you do choose to follow the above steps and, as a result, come up with any other tips drawn from your own personal wisdom, do use them to help yourself (and do let me know!).

Tips: Guru-worshipping – without Blind Following

❏ Don't expect one guru to give you all the answers to your life – have as *many* as you want and need to suit the different aspects of you, your various roles and interests.

❏ Hunt out your *own particular favourites*, don't just rely on the gurus you have been spoon fed by the media. Not all gurus like being centre-stage, and many 'leading edge' ones would not find a mass audience anyway. You may be more likely to find yours through specialist sections of libraries, galleries, etc.

❏ Search for signs that your guru is *practising what he or she preaches*.

❏ Choose gurus who *openly acknowledge a debt of gratitude to others*. The best gurus, in my experience, seem to have been guru-worshippers themselves at some stage and see their work and ideas as developments which can be partly attributed to the preceding centuries of others' insight and wisdom.

❏ Look for evidence which would suggest that these gurus are *not rigidly stuck in an ideological rut*. (That is, it should be obvious that they themselves are committed to ongoing change and self-development and can listen to new and opposing ideas.)

❏ Gurus can be *fantasy figures*. If you can't find a real person, dead or alive, to suit your purposes, make one up. It's not a crazy thing to do, in fact quite a natural one. Children quite spontaneously use imaginary friends or toys to fulfil various roles. Many years ago I went to a creative visualization therapy session which helped me create an imaginary figure of a wise person. I knew this 'person' had never existed and was made up of a concoction of my own subconscious wisdom, but he did feel real enough for me to 'consult' with him successfully (in my imagination) on many occasions.

❏ *Humanize* your mortal gurus by making personal contact with or seeing them in the flesh if you can (write a letter to them through their publishers/agent, hear them speak, etc.). If you cannot make personal contact, read their biography or autobiography, which will help bring them to life as real people. Awesome figures on pedestals tend to be disempowering rather than inspiring.

❏ Guidance from a guru in real life or in your imagination can be very supportive when you are wanting to make some difficult changes in your life and are lacking in motivation. But guru-worshipping should *never become an addiction* which controls you and the way you choose to live your life or undertake your challenges (that is, never reach a position where you feel that it would be literally *impossible* to start or carry on with a project without reference to your guru's ideas).

❏ When you have a particularly difficult decision to make, think through in your *mind's eye* what arguments or encouragement your guru(s) would give *you* (and not themselves in the same situation). Be careful not to let them make the decision for you, especially against your own better judgement.

❏ Always keep yourself in regular contact with *alternative ideas and approaches* to that which your guru teaches.

Instant Exercise:
Guru-worshipping –
without Blind Following

1 Think of four inspiring and high-achieving people
  whom you know or know of (they can be alive or dead).
2 Close your eyes and, after spending a couple of minutes
  relaxing your body, imagine these people are guests on a
  television panel to which you have sole confidential
  access. Ask them a few questions, using thoughts and
  queries which spontaneously pop into your head. Note
  whether there is any variation in their answers and ask
  yourself whether you agree with each.
3 Imagine that each of these people has been briefed by
  the researcher on some interesting aspects of your life
  and ideas, and now he or she is genuinely keen to ask
  you some questions! Keep up an imaginary discussion
  for the next five minutes.

*Today a hero is not so much one who sets an example for oth-
ers...heroes must be able to receive as well as give, because
influence which travels one way can become dispiriting or
corrupting.*

THEODORE ZELDIN

Driver 5

Sound Self-esteem – without Ignorant Arrogance

(Notebook page 218)

Loving myself enough to clear myself of continually outmoded attitudes and overwhelming fears has helped me to get to a place where I can honestly set down this personal and practical journey in book form.

BETTY CLARE MOFFATT –
When Someone You Love Has AIDS (PLUME, 1986)

 As I said in the introduction, my three dozen Drivers of the self-motivated are definitely not listed in order of importance. But if you were to force me into a corner and make me choose the most important, it would probably have to be this one.

Self-esteem is undoubtedly the life-blood of consistent long-lasting self-motivation. When it is thin and watery we have no resistance to excuses and setbacks, but when it is rich and healthy we can thrive on challenge even when there is no obvious sign of reward.

Ironically, lack of motivation can be the biggest hurdle to overcome for people who want more self-esteem! I have been running esteem-building courses now for very many years, and almost without exception I find that the toughest part of the job is convincing people at the outset that high self-esteem and arrogance are not only different but opposite. Until this has been achieved, any amount of brilliant or easy tips for building and boosting our sense of self-worth will fall on suspicious ears.

The fear of either being (or at least seeming) arrogant is understandably off-putting for most people. Pride is, after all, one of our culture's most deadly sins. But people whose self-esteem is high are never arrogant.

First, they do *not need to feel superior to other people* to feel good about themselves. Secondly, they do *not have any desire to be seen as better* than anyone else. The judgements which they prefer to make about themselves tend to concern their own potential. For example, if they have performed badly when they know that they should have done better, you can never comfort them with the news that others have done worse.

For my book *Self-Esteem* I listed all the main characteristics which I have observed in people who manage to maintain consistently high self-esteem. Since this book was published I have had the opportunity of talking to hundreds and hundreds of people from all walks of life and all ages on the subject. I have been told that this list has proved to be a very useful yardstick by which you can measure your *current degree of self-esteem*. So I am including it below in the form of a Checklist. Why not, as you read it, mark each characteristic with a grading on a scale of 1 – 10?

Checklist: Characteristics of a Person with High Self-esteem

- ❏ generally relaxed, self-composed manner
- ❏ rewarding and balanced lifestyle
- ❏ well-nourished and well-exercised body
- ❏ enjoys being productive and has firm belief in own ability to make a contribution
- ❏ openly shares pride in own strengths, personal satisfactions and achievements
- ❏ communicates directly and expressively
- ❏ comfortable in own company and capable of self-direction
- ❏ harmonious social relationships, can work collaboratively
- ❏ sound sense of values and lives a life which reflects these
- ❏ proactive and assertive in relation to own needs

- ❏ welcomes constructive criticism and keen to learn from mistakes
- ❏ self-reflective and eager to develop own potential
- ❏ willing to give encouragement and support to others

You may be interested to note that lack of self-esteem is no longer something with which just low-achievers suffer, it seems it is now *hurting the successful* and their motivation as well. So if your score was lower than you would like to have seen (e.g. several falling below seven out of ten) remind yourself that this could unfortunately be more a sign of the times than any cause for you to feel bad about yourself.

High achievers, for all sorts of reasons, have recently become both much more self-reflective and idealistic. Perhaps this is one of the reasons why so many have begun to judge themselves to be unworthy of the rewards which their success has brought, and less motivated to work at their goals. Perhaps another is that in this fast-paced changing world of today's workplace, they (like so many others) have not been getting enough boosts and support to counter-balance the knocks and setbacks that have so inevitably accompanied the recession and the remodelling of organizations. Formerly, as people climbed the ladder, even if the challenges became harder the symbols of success and the 'kow-towing' of subordinates were perhaps sufficient to nurture their egos.

But in the most successful and confident of modern workplaces, self-sustainable high self-esteem is now considered a prerequisite for any responsible job. Limousines and exclusive restaurants are increasingly regarded as 'unnecessary' perks, and fawning and grovelling have already become dying arts. The self-worth of everyone from the managing director to the window cleaner is expected to be impervious to the cold, cutting criticism of performance appraisals and competitive colleagues.

In the world of the wider community, traditional forms of external esteem-boosting are also on the decrease. Even society's most respected and highly qualified professionals such as doctors, teachers and politicians (not to mention archbishops and royalty!) and the heroes of TV, sport and pop music can no longer rely on their titles, qualifications or success to help them feel good about themselves. The days when shaky self-confidence could be shored up by the outer trappings of success are gone. Even our finest heroes now have their egos constantly challenged by an increasingly irreverent and iconoclastic media.

So none of us can rely on achievement alone to give adequate support to our self-esteem. The following tips (plus any others you can lay your hands on) should therefore be kept not just for those demotivating rainy days, but also to keep the sun inwardly shining during your moments of success!

 # Tips: Sound Self-esteem – without Ignorant Arrogance

- ❏ Use the *Characteristics Checklist* (*page 24*) once a month until your self-esteem remains consistently high over a six-month period. After completing it, write down a specific statement of commitment to improve your self-esteem (for example, 'This month I will be committed to replying assertively to any put-downs which come my way' / 'This month I will commit more time to exercise,' etc.).
- ❏ Each time your self-esteem receives a knock, take care to *repair it appropriately* (for example, a disappointing exam result may call for a drink with an understanding friend, and a forgotten birthday may merit a present for yourself). Remember that unrepaired small knocks do chip away at your self-esteem and lower your resistance to the bigger ones.
- ❏ Each time you give yourself a challenge where there is a reasonable risk of failure (applying for a new job or tendering for a contract, asking a highly desirable person for a date, or even asking a busy colleague for a favour), make sure that you have planned a *compensatory treat* for yourself as a back-up.

❏ *Never highlight your weaknesses* unnecessarily ('Thanks for the compliment, I am surprised you like it, because I think it draws attention to my short arms' / 'You may notice that I have a tendency to speak too quietly').

❏ Make a habit of *sharing your successes* with people who will be genuinely pleased for you and not secretly envious (tell a friend rather than a low-achieving competitive colleague about a difficult deal you managed to clinch, or someone at the gym about your lost kilos rather than a fellow weight-watcher).

❏ Like the Scouts, check that each day you do at least *one good deed* which offers no reward other than an inner boost to your own self-worth (holding a door open for a stranger; making an anonymous donation; checking an elderly neighbour has brought her milk in; picking up a piece of litter).

 # Instant Exercise: Sound Self-esteem – without Ignorant Arrogance

1 Write down six personal qualities (not skills) in yourself which you admire.
2 Write down three weaknesses which you are currently successfully correcting (for example, I am controlling my greed for chocolate; I am now much less sarcastic; I am much better at time-keeping than I was this time last year).
3 Put this book down for a moment and give yourself an instant treat (even if you can only spare five minutes breathing space!).

Just trust yourself and you will know how to live.

GOETHE

Driver 6

Thirst for Challenge — without Scorning Easy Options

(Notebook page 218)

> *This is the true joy in life, the being used for a purpose recognized by yourself as a mighty one...instead of [being] a selfish little clod of ailments and grievances complaining that the world will not devote itself to making you happy.*
>
> GEORGE BERNARD SHAW

 'Why do I always make life so difficult for myself?'
This is a question I used to ask myself repeatedly. But, like all expert self-saboteurs, I didn't really want to hear the answer. I just wanted to hear a justification for my hard life! The 'crazy' style of self-talk I used to reassure myself went something like this:

'That's just the way you are. Yes you're a born masochist, but wouldn't you be bored if your life *wasn't* full of hurdles? Without pressure you'd never do anything. Anyway, the truth is that life *is* hard and anything worth having always involves struggle.'

Often I would have my reassurance reinforced by 'Ain't it hard, but aren't *we* wonderful?' conversations with friends. Perhaps you can recognize some of the familiar phrases we'd use:

'Oh I know what you mean, I'm my own worst enemy too.'

'I wish I were more like —. I suppose we just weren't destined for an easy life...no silver spoons for sinners like us...I must have done something very wrong in my last life...it firms up your character, though...at least we didn't take things for granted...but the harder things are to get, the more we enjoy them, don't we?'

We'd carry on until we'd convinced each other that not only were easy options impossible for people like us but also that our struggling 'elite' wouldn't want them if they were offered to us!

Of course, these kinds of 'games', whether they are played inside or outside of our heads, are not only CRAZY – they are also very demotivational.

So why do so many of us do it? It could be caused by a number of different factors, such as:

– a bad contagious cultural habit. Most people who have been brought up in the stoical 'cold showers are good for you' climate of Great Britain have some of this crazy thinking lurking in their collective subconscious.
– a religious belief which convinces that the harder this life is the better the next one will be, because struggle is an atonement for sin.
– an overdose of messages from parents and other role-models who maintained that 'hard work never did me any harm...the trouble with the world today is that young people have it too easy.'
– unresolved grief or guilt from a past 'easy option' which didn't work out favourably.
– justification for under-achievement due to laziness or lack of confidence.

Once I began to realize where my crazy philosophy had developed, I began to understand (and prove!) that often I could have my cake and take great pleasure in eating and sharing it as well! A good example of how I took the upper hand on this bad habit was the way we bought our house in southern Spain.

My husband and I both thrive on challenge, so it was very much in keeping with our characters to choose to look for a farmhouse in a remote country village in spite of the fact that our DIY skills are virtually zero-rated and our budget exceedingly limited. We'd read books on buying property in Spain and we talked to friends who 'knew all about it' and we prepared ourselves for not just years of scrimping and saving, but also interminable battles with bureaucracy and con artists. The only thing I wasn't ready for was the mental struggle which I encountered when the *easy* option came our way!

A few months after our decision, my husband was casually glancing through the Sunday paper when he spotted a tiny advert for an amazingly affordable property in Andalusia. On the spur of the moment we sent for details, arranged a cheap flight and set off. In the space of much less than one week we had signed the deal that realized our dream.

But it was all so easy that I nearly sabotaged our success with my negative thinking. As we approached the hotel where we had arranged to do the signing, the panic and prejudice started. 'There's something wrong here,' I thought – '*it's all too easy*. You can't buy a house in a matter of days – it takes months if not years of looking to find the right one – this *Spanish* solicitor – he's too nice and too helpful...how do I know he's properly qualified? How can I believe this man who wants to sell...is his story believable? What proof do I have that he's not out to con me? The house looks too good to be true – the foundations must be crumbling. The people in the village are so friendly and welcoming...they must see some easy foreign money coming...*the whole thing is going too smoothly – there must be a catch.*'

Thank goodness the (relatively new) positive me won this inner struggle. I accepted that we had encountered a stroke of luck and we had checked it out to the very best of our ability, so we seized upon this chance and set off to satisfy our thirst for challenge elsewhere!

Since that time I have been much more consciously on the lookout for 'lucky breaks' and easy options. Needless to say I have found many, and not only do I enjoy the experience of taking them, I find that they inspire me to cope with challenges as well.

Tips: Thirst for Challenge – without Scorning Easy Options

❏ Remember that challenges are only motivational if the odds *permit you to win* sometimes.
❏ Check with yourself that your challenges are *enjoyable and stimulating,* not just 'rods for your back.'
❏ Mix with *people who have a passion* for challenges and who use them positively.
❏ Read inspiring books and watch biographical films about *people who have won battles* against extremely difficult odds (such as *Children of a Lesser God, Schindler's List, Lust for Life, Gandhi, Cry Freedom*).
❏ Make a conscious effort to be on the *look-out for easy options* and lucky breaks.
❏ Use *affirmations and support* from positive thinkers to beat any 'old messages' from your inner negative demon.
❏ Remind yourself constantly that *success is built on an astute ability to synchronize challenge and chance.*

Instant Exercise: Thirst for Challenge – without Scorning Easy Options

1 Think of one or two challenges you have overcome in your life and note down the personal qualities you used to help you surmount these.
2 Ask yourself if your current lifestyle gives you enough opportunity to exercise these personal qualities. If not, make a resolution and plan now!
3 Think of another challenge you have had in the past with which you did not cope quite as well. Ask yourself if, with hindsight, you could have made the struggle any easier for yourself (for example by asking for help, researching the facts, being more positive).

Self-motivation

We don't really work at our best unless there are obstacles to overcome.

WALT DISNEY

Driver 7

Addiction to Achievement – without Imprudent Impatience

(Notebook page 219)

> *It is very strange that the years teach us patience...the shorter our time, the greater our capacity for waiting.*
>
> ELIZABETH TAYLOR

 All high achievers know how intensely addictive the 'peak experience' feeling can be. When we reach our challenging goals, the physical and emotional state of ecstasy we find ourselves in can even render us temporarily irrational. Like all other addicts, we may find ourselves *wanting more success than we actually need*, and becoming increasingly tempted by dubious quick-fixes or short-term gains.

Unfortunately, although (as we have already discussed) we may from time to time on the road to success be lucky enough to meet a few short-cuts, I do not know any consistent achievers who would count on chance to keep them motivated. Most accept that long-lasting strength is built *step by step* and that, especially in the early foundation stages, an *endless supply of patience* is often required. The preparatory tasks of clarifying principles, setting clear goals and making detailed action plans (not to mention mustering scarce resources!) can last depressingly longer than most of us would wish. I know that these are the times which are a true test of the mettle of my own self-motivation.

I don't believe that the high achievers who seem to sail through these early trials and other frustratingly slow stretches *en route* to their goals were born with above-average patience. In fact, quite the reverse is usually true. I have found most have a very low threshold of boredom and hate 'waiting around in the wings' before the exciting action begins to move forward again. *Patience is usually one of those personal qualities that most addicts of high achievement have to nurture and consistently maintain.* Like me, they have often had to learn about its advantages the hard way, and have a history of mistakes that could have been avoided, created by their own impatience.

Hopefully, if you follow some of these tips you may be able to avoid some of the expensive (and demotivating) setbacks my own 'Hurry-up' Driver has brought to bear upon on some of my projects!

 # Tips: Addiction to Achievement – without Imprudent Impatience

❏ Don't waste time trying to view patience as a virtue and your impatience as a sin that must be punished. *Replace self-kicks and put-downs* with more digestible statements of 'fact' (such as, 'patience is a *necessary* evil; patience is a quality which I can choose to nurture and then use from *time to time*'!).

❏ Keep a *list* of small (but still very worthwhile) jobs (in a file, in your diary or in your head) which can easily be worked on during odd periods which might be normally wasted. (Robert Anthony, author of *Doing What You Love and Loving What You Do*, calls these periods *scrap time*. He points out that ten minutes a day of using idle moments adds up to one 40-hour working week in a year! In financial terms alone, it should be easy to calculate the value of that kind of time either to you or to the company which employs you.)

❏ Never 'watch your pots boil'. Develop the habit of using *waiting time* productively. (For example, revive your vision with some purposeful daydreaming; reflect on your overall progress; rehearse in your head a difficult phone call you need to make – or just calmly repeat patience-affirming statements!)

❏ Always be prepared with stimulating things to do *en route* before setting off on any of your *journeys*. Make sure that you also have extra interesting activities or relaxation aids you could slot in if you are held up (a new cassette for the traffic jam; letter-writing tools for the station waiting room or your Christmas card list [plus an inflatable pillow!] for the airport departure lounge).

❏ Use meditation or other relaxation techniques *regularly* to quiet and *control your 'Hurry-up' Driver* and recharge you for the next step.

❏ Use your *assertive skills* (*see page 136*) to stop anyone else from 'pushing' you to move faster than you know is advisable.

Instant Exercise: Addiction to Achievement – without Imprudent Impatience

• Put down this book. For the next ten minutes use this unexpected piece of 'scrap time' in any of the ways I have suggested above. Whether you use it for some action towards your goals or for relaxation must be your decision, but check that you are using it constructively as part of your plan to develop your self-motivation.

Patience is the knot which secures the seam of victory.
CHINESE PROVERB

Steadfast Principles – without Narrow Prejudice

(Notebook page 219)

> *It's easier to fight for one's principles than to live up to them.*
> ALFRED ADLER

 Deeply embedded in the hearts of successful self-motivators you will always find a set of guiding principles. Their lives have not just a sense of purpose, but a sense of *moral* purpose. Having a grasp on what they believe is right and wrong is very important to them. Even though they may have no illusions about their 'sanctity', they know that working against their code of ethics not only makes them feel uncomfortable, it also restricts their potential. This is one of the main reasons why so many of the self-motivators whom I have met chose self-employment in the 1980s working culture. Many left the 'rat race' not because they did not like racing, but because they felt demotivated being a rat!

Fortunately today's mainstream working culture seems to be changing. If you glance around the bookshelves of any section on management and organizational development, you will notice that many of the new titles and chapter headings reflect the growing interest in values. What self-respecting company would now want to operate in today's climate without its mission statement?

> *The most effective competitors in the 21st century will be the organizations that learn how to use shared values to harness the emotional energy of employees.*
>
> NOEL M. TICHY AND STRATFORD SHERMAN

I am not naïve enough to think that this concern for values has been prompted by pure altruism. There is no doubt that without the customer's new assertive demands for improved quality and the competitive state of today's recession-ridden business world, we would not be hearing so many companies talking in these new terms.

But, on the other hand, in recent years I have had the privilege of talking (usually in complete confidence) to many senior managers and directors, and there is no doubt that there is a genuine concern not just to be seen to be ethical, but to square their practices with their consciences. These quotes from senior managers and directors illustrate this:

'What's the point of slogging my heart out when I have no genuine pride in what I am achieving? I never intended to "sell-out" – it's just the way things worked out. It seemed the only way to get the mortgage paid.'

'I have worked at the expense of both my health and my personal life all these years and now I am wondering why. It wasn't always money that was driving me, I just got caught up in a race and had lost sight of the goal posts. I suppose I was just following in my father's footsteps. I admired him but I'm different.'

'I know it's a waste of my skills, but I'm thinking of taking early retirement and buying a shop. I don't mind hard work but I know I don't want to spend the rest of my life working for principles which I don't approve of.'

'I'm sure some people would say I'm after a knighthood – I just want to feel as though what I am doing is making a difference to the world and not just lining my own and the shareholders' pockets.'

'I've never been afraid of power, but now I have achieved it, the big question is can I square my conscience with the decisions I find I have to make? I wasn't short of motivation until

I got to the top, but now...I am beginning to wonder if I'm in the right job after all.'

Fortunately, a life crisis and subsequent personal development work forced me to do some similar hard moral self-questioning 20 years ago. As a result, it became clear that an important 'mission' for me was to make a contribution to the *prevention* of mental health problems. I knew that I was not averse to making money (in fact, I *love* the freedom it can give me and my family), but in my list of working principles I had to face the fact that financial gain was at the lower end of *my* motivating principles list.

It was then that I came face to face with the crunch 'moral' decision. I knew that in my line of business at that time (social work), because resources were scarce and clients relatively poor, investment was unlikely to be put into the 'non-crisis' area of work which *I* deemed to be important. At that time there seemed no alternative but to keep myself away from the mainstream ladders of working success in my field. I forced myself to stop scouring the tempting adverts for senior management posts and chose to work for a new penniless charity and my own low-return business. I wasn't being a martyr looking for a halo, I was merely seeking work which was satisfying and stimulating for me.

I have never for one minute regretted this choice because I have subsequently developed a career path which I thoroughly enjoy and feel highly dedicated to and motivated to pursue. The fact that I am constantly assured that my work does make a difference to others' lives has, I know, inspired me through many a rough, tough patch.

But, I am well aware that if I had been in a different line of business my choice of guiding principles might have been very different. You, for example, may be lucky enough to be doing work which offers you the opportunity to make a fortune as well as a difference!

Alternatively, financial gain may not even be an issue in what you are trying to achieve. This might be true if, perhaps, you are reading this book because you are keen to improve your motivation to diet more strictly, play darts more professionally, or campaign for a cause more consistently. You may find yourself choosing from among other kinds of principles such as quality and quantity, or speed/efficiency and ecology.

Once we have established our own core principles, we enter a danger zone! This is a land where high-mindedness, prejudice and intolerance *can* thrive. This is particularly true if your work or activity is mainly self-directed and you are not regularly forced to defend and possibly reappraise your principles with others who hold differing views. As I enjoy a good argument, I find debating my values and having some of my prejudices regularly challenged excellent ways of recharging the moral part of me. I usually leave such exchanges feeling more inspired and more determined. Other people prefer less confrontational methods of keeping a check on their moral bias.

In the tips and exercise which follow, I hope you will find some suggestions which will help you not only to firm up your sense of dedication but also to keep your resistance to prejudice unyielding.

Tips: Steadfast Principles –
without Narrow Prejudice

❑ Before starting any new project, concisely list your *working principles*. Don't be afraid of making them sound too lofty. Err on the side of piousness – it's better for your motivation to have a moral purpose to look up and not down on!

❑ Before starting *any* project which requires your collaboration, be sure to elicit other people's principles and assess whether you *can* have a *workable consensus*. (This may mean asking some awkward questions at a job interview or a first committee or board meeting – so take good note of the next Driver and firm up your courage!).

❑ Be *strictly honest* with yourself. Keep a clear distinction between your *core* values – i.e. the ones which you would never bend (such as earning enough money to keep your

children fed and housed; maintaining your health)
and your more *flexible* ones (such as fairness; quality
of product; keeping promises).

❏ Test out the *current validity* of your principles regularly.
Do this by taking the Devil's advocate position yourself.
(You can use two chairs facing each other, each
representing the opposite value, and argue your case
out by sitting on each in turn. Alternatively, write out
two lists, one of 'points in favour' and the other 'points
against').

❏ Keep yourself *regularly informed* of other people's points
of view (by, for example, reading the books on mission
statements in Section 4 of this book; occasionally buying
newspapers of the opposite political leaning to your own;
watching TV debates and from time to time seeing films
on subjects which would normally never interest you).

 **Instant Exercise: Steadfast Principles
– without Narrow Prejudice**

1 List three core values (in hierarchical order) for two
projects with which you are involved. One could be a
work project and another could be personal.
2 Write down the name of a 'stimulating someone' with
whom you could discuss these and your other more
flexible values in the not-too-distant future.

*It's easy to have principles when you are rich. The important
thing is to have principles when you are poor.*

RAY CROC

Consistent Courage – without Thoughtless Gambling

(Notebook page 220)

> *Fortune does not favour the sensitive amongst us: it smiles on the audacious, who are not afraid to say 'The die is cast.'*
>
> ERASMUS

 After the Self-esteem Driver (5), this must be the next most important one for me. After all, courage underpins so many of the other Drivers we are working on.

Doesn't it take courage to:

– share the vision of your dream when others may not believe it can be realized?
– declare your neediness, when others may scorn you for doing so?
– be decisive when you know you *could* be wrong?
– be proactive when the world outside your 'comfort zone' looks tough?
– stick to your principles when others appear to be flourishing on a diet of opposing values?
– deal with your emotions when your pain is surfacing?
– keep self-motivated when others around you have lost heart?

But the good news is that, ironically, many of the other Drivers can in turn help you *control* your fear! For example, knowing what is important for you gives your courage a boost and helps you to stand up for your rights, and regularly sharing your goals with certain friends can keep your natural timidity at bay.

Courage is a quality which is so socially acceptable that I am sure you do not need much more convincing of its value. But, like self-esteem, in the competitive and often harsh world of today it also has a tendency to ebb and flow. Even the lions among the super-self-motivators quake from time to time. (Hidden in the agenda of many stress-management programmes for senior executives you will now find modules on managing fear!) So don't feel a wimp for needing to seek out courage-building opportunities. But when you do so, be careful of the ones which encourage taking very great risks. These can be counter-productive. In my opinion, courage is a strength which thrives on being built up step by step. The 'plunging in at the deep end' approach has been responsible for demotivating so many people whom I know personally, that I admit to being totally prejudiced against it.

If you still feel short on courage after following my tips, there is plenty of other reading you can do. Susan Jeffers, Clair Weekes and Dorothy Rowe are all excellent authors on the subject. (*Their books and many others are listed in Section 4.*)

Tips: Consistent Courage – without Thoughtless Gambling

❏ Remind yourself regularly that, however desirable courage is, it is not a sign of a superior being. It is a *natural quality* which every one of us was born with to ensure both our own growth and the continuance of planet earth. Those who have less of it by the time they reach adulthood have merely had more fear with which to contend. By learning to take control f your response to fear, you can reclaim your full quota of natural courage. So it is now *your choice* whether you have more or less of it than anyone else.

❏ Never try to deny your fear. As with handling all negative emotions, one of the tricks is to *allow yourself to feel* the feelings, but only to the extent that you remain in control. If, as a result of your past you have a store of pre-conditioned fear responses, it helps to assure your subconscious regularly of the new state of affairs (use an affirmation such as: 'I acknowledge that I'm feeling fear but I am courageous and can control it').

❏ While always striving to put your toe a little further into the water, *never take on more fear than* you *have judged is controllable* by your current store of courage. Let others support and encourage you, but firmly draw the line at them telling you what you are, or are not, feeling (for example, '*You* can't be frightened of that').

❏ Before taking a risk, always try to imagine and face the *worst possible outcome*. Prepare a contingency plan (*see example on page 162*). It is not courageous but cowardly to say to yourself 'I'll cross that bridge when I come to it.'

❏ Use breathing exercises and meditation techniques to *calm your physical symptoms* as soon as they appear. (You will find several tried and tested techniques in my book *Self-esteem*.)

❑ Use *creative visualization* to give yourself an extra boost of courage the night before a difficult risk (again, this technique is fully explained in *Self-esteem* and several other books in my reading list and on my tapes).

❑ Courage is a quality which can undoubtedly go rusty without *constant exercise*, so make sure that you have plenty of practice in your everyday life. For example, practise using your courage thoughtfully to make the suggestions you want to make at meetings in spite of the possibility that they might get laughed or sneered at; approach interesting looking people whom you'd like to have a conversation with, even though you haven't been introduced; wear clothes which may turn a few heads and get you noticed even by people you'd prefer were not around!

 Instant Exercise: Consistent Courage – without Thoughtless Gambling

1 Take some time to reflect on your experiences of both courage and gambling, and recall the physical sensations which you experienced. (There is a fine line, which is different for each of us, between the excitement of a courageous self-motivator and an over-anxious fool and potential coward! Your *body* rather than your head can usually tell you best when you have reached this line).

2 Make a note of the signs in *your* body which indicate you are on that fine line (for me it is a sick feeling in the pit of my stomach and sensations of slight constriction and dryness in my throat).

The mouse that hath but one hole is quickly taken.

PROVERB

Driver 10

Endless Energy –
without Debilitating Burnout

(Notebook page 220)
  'How do you do it?'
  'How on earth do you fit it all in?'
  'Where do you get your energy from?'
These are questions which I am asked so regularly that I must accept that I do maintain above-average levels of energy even though I am constantly aware that I would like (and know I could have!) so much more.

> *At 74 I sold, for the sum of 2 million dollars, my fried chicken business, which I'd started at the age of 65, when I was getting ready to live out my days on Social Security.*
>
> COLONEL SANDERS

 What I do find easier to acknowledge is that I certainly do (like Colonel Sanders!) have a very much greater supply of energy now than I did in the Spring of my youth. Ironically, it was a spell of 'premature burnout' during that period of my life to which I now owe most thanks for my current stamina.

For the first 15 years of my adult life, I habitually burned my candle in the middle as well as at both ends. In a mistaken attempt to energize my body I filled it regularly with stimulating toxins such as alcohol, nicotine, strong coffee and antidepressants. When it needed sleep I knocked it out with barbiturates and hallucinogens. In the mean time I was building up a chronic supply of muscle tension caused by overdoses of mismanaged sadness, frustration and anger. And, apart from wild drunken rock-and-roll sessions, neither exercise nor sport ever had a place on my agenda.

Needless to say I always felt tired and I was constantly beset with minor infections. The company I kept (mainly from the media and caring professions) were no shining examples of good self-care, either. Even though our educated heads should have known better, we supported and encouraged self-destructiveness in each other.

Eventually, under the extra strain of two young children, a job and a major crisis in my first marriage, my body went into rapid decline. I won't bore you (or me) with the details of my various complaints. It is sufficient to say that they were serious enough to shock and frighten me. I realized that at least for the sake of my two daughters, I had to change my ways drastically.

Fortunately, a gift of a ten-day spell in a health farm broke up my negative patterns and gave me a taste of the long-forgotten buzz which high energy can give. I wish I could sign a prescription for all my clients to have the same experience before commencing their personal development work. Not only did it give my body a much-needed boost, it helped me to *accept nurturing and care from others* and also gave me a *peaceful period in which to reflect creatively about my life and its priorities*. In my absence my problems had not evaporated, but I did return to them more invigorated and inspired and was therefore much more able and willing to solve them.

Since that time, neither my budget nor my lifestyle has allowed me to repeat this experience, but I have made sure that I put the life-saving lessons it taught me into *almost* daily use. It hasn't been easy because (like most self-motivated people!) I am definitely inclined in the direction of workaholism and have not yet developed a passion for physical workouts!

The following tips, therefore, should be ignored by those of you who are enviably more dedicated to a laid-back lifestyle and physical fitness. But I am assuming that at least some of my readers can empathize with my difficulties and will read them (and put them to use) avidly!

You can redirect your life as soon as you decide that you are sick and tired of being sick and tired.

DR ROBERT ANTHONY

Tips: Endless Energy – without Debilitating Burnout

❑ Go green with your own energy – view it as a scarce resource, to be valued and used economically. *Conserve* it whenever you can, so you have plenty left for your important projects (for example, if you have to travel, consider going by train instead of tiring yourself out driving; assertively refuse to do things that you don't need or wish to do).

❑ Remember: stress eats away energy faster than almost anything else. Get to know and keep a short list of your own *personal warning signals* of stress (such as: Body – backache; headaches; stomach upsets, etc. Obsessive behaviour – skipping meals; driving too fast, etc.; Emotions – irritability; excitability; apathy, etc. A full Checklist can be found in my book, *Self-esteem*).

❑ Rather than imposing a punishing ban on de-energizing foods and drinks, cut them down and *strictly limit your intake* to certain periods of the day. While you are working, take nutritious snacks rather than big meals.

❑ If you are mostly chair-bound when working, take regular short breaks in which you physically release your tension, pumping up the energy of your body and mind (stretching, short aerobic exercises and meditation all help).

❑ Use the *rhythm of your own energy cycles* to your best advantage (for example, I know that mine are low mid-afternoon, so I arrange my life so that siestas are usually possible – my programme of evening commitments justifies me taking them!).

❏ Keep your *creative tasks for times when you have most energy*, and your 'spade work' for other times (though I myself still have to resist strenuously the temptation to get my administrative and housework tasks 'over with' in the morning even though I know that this is the very best time for me to start writing or planning).

❏ Remember only *certain* changes can be as good as a rest; most are extremely high on energy-consumption and you will need to make a big *allowance* for this fact.

 # Instant Exercise: Endless Energy – without Debilitating Burnout

1 Knowing your current lifestyle and habits, in percentage terms rate your chances of developing 'burnout' within the next 20 years. (A definition of burnout in this context would be: being prematurely physically and mentally exhausted to the extent that you are no longer able to use your potential.)

2 Write down three simple things you plan to do differently *as of tomorrow morning* to decrease this score and increase your energy levels.

Driver 11

Prepared Proactivity – without Disregard for Opportunity

(Notebook page 221)

> *One should act before anyone else has a chance to react.*
> BARON PHILIPPE DE ROTHSCHILD

 Proactivity (that is, initiating activity) is so obvious an essential quality in any self-motivator's 'tool-kit' that I am sure I do not need to sing its praises to convince you. You wouldn't be reading this if you intended to let yourself become the kind of person whose reminiscences in old age are full of regrets for the actions he or she did *not* initiate.

But maybe you would like to improve your ability to use your inclination for proactivity more skilfully. In my experience, those who use this quality to 'change their world' constructively act in specific ways. I have devised the following mnemonic to illustrate the key steps which can make being proactive so useful:

Prepare
Rest
Organize
Act
Calculate
Try again

Let me explain each of these steps with some examples:

Prepare

Successful self-motivators:

- *think hard* (if not necessarily for long) before they act.
- do enough research (and no more than enough) in the field they are planning to operate in, to assure themselves that they will not be wasting their precious energy on projects and ideas which have been sufficiently tried and tested and found to be 'wanting'. (But of course they are not put off if they think they have a *new* approach.)
- often carefully *script out* their opening requests and rehearse them to ensure that they will have the greatest possible impact (such as their requests to their politician, union representative, the board or even Mum!).

Rest

Successful self-motivators:
- are aware that being proactive requires their *full quota of energy levels*, so they do not try to initiate projects or action when their reserves are low. They take good quality rest *before starting* to ensure that they make the best use of their proactivity.

Organize

Successful self-motivators:
- do not start without checking that they can make enough *extra time* for the project. They do not kid themselves that they will be able to 'make time' from thin air, however interesting a new idea might be. They organize their diaries in advance.
- realize that while they are in proactive mode they may not have the same time and attention to give to routine tasks and responsibilities, so they organize for these duties to be *well looked after* while they are distracted.
- make sure that they have *sufficient resources* to meet any

foreseeable expenditure and have enough in reserve for the inevitable unforeseen expenses of any new project. They never rely on the vagaries of a lottery win to bail them out of difficulty!

Act

Successful self-motivators:

– love this exciting stage of new purposeful decisive and assertive action. The difference between them and many other initiators is that they *do not rush to this stage* or get stuck in the excitement of this position. They know when it is time to move on to the next stages.

Calculate

Successful self-motivators:

– stand back and *reflect* objectively on their proactive action.
– ask for honest, critical *feedback*.
– take careful note of the *facts and figures*.
– use their experience and new information to re-evaluate the costing of the project in terms of *resources* such as money and time.

Try Again

Successful self-motivators:

– don't give up after the shock of the last step! They give their self-motivational drivers a boost and get themselves into the proactive cycle yet *again*!

I hope you will find this mnemonic helpful when exercising your proactive skills, but I also hope that you won't get so enthusiastically involved in your particular new project that you do not notice the other opportunities around you.

To make sure that this does not happen, it may be important to keep scheduled in your timetable occasions when you can do this specifically. I know that when I'm involved in an exciting new venture which I have initiated, I sometimes have to force myself to make time to continue keeping myself actively open to other new ideas. It is so much easier in the short term to don my blinkers and isolate myself while I am getting going. Adopting this kind of approach when we are being proactive is now a luxury few of us can afford. The world is moving so fast that we cannot afford to be cut off from new possibilities for long.

All good things come to those who wait, but only what's left behind by those who seized the opportunities.

ABRAHAM LINCOLN

Tips: Prepared Proactivity – without Disregard for Opportunity

❏ *Write out the PROACT mnemonic on a card* and carry it around with you for a while. Read it regularly until you have learned it off by heart.

❏ If ever you hear yourself say the words *'If only ...'*, stop, get out your card and consider whether you could instead take some proactive steps.

❏ When initiative feels very hard to come by, immediately ask yourself these *questions*:
(a) 'Can I afford *not* to be proactive in this situation?
(b) 'What is likely to be the cost in the long term of not taking action today?'

❏ Never turn down any opportunity to be proactive just because the idea has been tried out before. With increased self-motivation it may work the second (or tenth!) time around.

❏ Keep your opportunity net as wide as your time will allow (for example, keep up some contact with all the organizations involved in your 'line'; don't just confine yourself to one group for networking, join several.)

Instant Exercise:
Prepared Proactivity –
without Disregard for Opportunity

1 Imagine that you have only three more weeks to live.
   Think what regrets you might begin to have. Ask yourself
   what proactive action you would like to have taken.
2 In the light of these thoughts, make a commitment to
   yourself to look actively for opportunities to be more
   proactive. (Set yourself a specific objective if you can
   at this stage.)

He who has begun has half done. Dare to be wise; begin!

HORACE

Driver 12

Solid Responsibility –
without Rigid Perfectionism

(Notebook page 221)

Nothing contributes so much to tranquilize the mind as a steady purpose.

MARY WOLLSTONECRAFT SHELLEY

 Nowadays all forward-thinking employers want a highly self-motivated workforce. It's not just that they can no longer afford expensive motivational treats and perks. It's because the point where the 'buck stops' is moving rapidly down the hierarchy. In flattened organizations, delegation is no longer an option for senior managers and directors, it is a necessity. They want self-motivated staff because they need them. They must now have more and more people on whom they can depend to take responsibility willingly.

Apart from being able to rely on them to get on with their own everyday work, they need people who can also, for example, accept responsibility for:

– their own feelings and self-care during times of uncomfortable change
– coping with the aggression they may stir up when their proactivity 'rocks the boat'
– the mistakes that they will obviously need to make in order to keep moving forward and learning

So big business is now weeding out those who have a tendency to throw responsibility outwards and rarely inwards, and these employees are being thrown into the world of self-employment and small business. But there is even less room in these worlds for these types of people. These fields require more, not less, responsibility.

But for some people, it is very much easier to accept and live according to the rule that if we 'make our bed we must also lie on it.' Through no fault of their own, they may have had their personality moulded into an irresponsible style. Deeply ingrained into their subconscious minds there are certain beliefs which *feel* like unshakeable truths:

– They feel convinced that they need to be told exactly what to do if ever they are going to do anything worth doing.
– They believe they will always need to be chased up before they can complete anything.
– They are convinced they were 'born lazy' and need that fault to be constantly controlled.

In the course of my career as both a social worker and therapist I have met many thousands of people who genuinely (and often secretly) held these kinds of beliefs about themselves because, perhaps:

– They were *not given enough opportunity* to develop responsibility for themselves (doting parents doing too much for them or lazy/over-worked teachers spoonfeeding them with exam answers instead of making them think).
– They discovered that the most efficient way of getting their needs met was to *'play helpless and dependent'* (perhaps the adults around them thrived on playing 'rescuing hero' or 'martyr nurse' roles).
– They were forced to *take responsibility too young* and didn't handle it well (or thought they didn't), and as a result developed the idea that they are 'no good at it'.
– Their parents, through their low-achieving example and even their 'direct teaching', gave them the *impression that*

there is no point in being responsible (that is, in adopting more adult behaviours and attitudes) because 'it doesn't get you anywhere in the end.'
– Their parents or influential peers may have *actively encouraged* them to be irresponsible (for example by smiling at their 'naughty twinkle' or mischievous behaviour).
– They were brought up in a culture where *anti-social behaviour was the norm* and their heroes were the ones who were most irresponsible (gang leaders; clever con-men; unscrupulous businesspeople; 'dodgy' dealers, etc.).

But, only a small minority of such people *'behave'* irresponsibly, in fact the majority are quite the opposite. Many, instead, behave *too responsibly*. At great expense to their mental health and the development of their potential, *they become perfectionists as a direct result of trying to control the 'lazy, irresponsible' part of themselves.* (Psychological defence mechanisms such as this usually first develop as survival skills in early childhood, and without correction become lifelong habits.)

As standards of perfection are rarely achievable, such people constantly feel failures and get depressed, or compulsively punish themselves with obvious self-destructive behaviour. This could sometimes take a conspicuous form as in the case of alcoholism, agoraphobia, anorexia or bulimia, though many other people adopt more 'socially acceptable' forms of behaviour such as workaholism, secret demeaning fetishes, involvement in persistently non-nurturing relationships or 'martyr' parenting.

Because society rewards perfectionism, these kinds of people are not necessarily low-achievers and they often wield great power. So once in their positions of power (teachers, matrons, managers, clergy, politicians, sergeant majors, consultant physicians, judges and many others!) they are able to force their perfectionism on hundreds of others.

Now you may be thinking, 'Surely these groups of people are usually the champions of responsibility and are held up as shining examples of self-motivation?' You would be right, of course. But they are 'wolves in sheep's clothing'. Their drive is entirely controlled by the prop of their perfectionism. If they lose this prop, through for example having a secret irresponsible habit publicly exposed, being made redundant or being defeated by rebellion, they often crumble into the self-destructive behaviours which I described earlier.

So, hopefully you can see why it is so important to get the balance of this Driver right. Because of my early childhood experiences I have always had a problem with it, and have had to work hard to control my own tendency to veer towards the three corners of the triangle below. The successful self-motivator needs to maintain a balance of all three. I hope these tips will help you to do this.

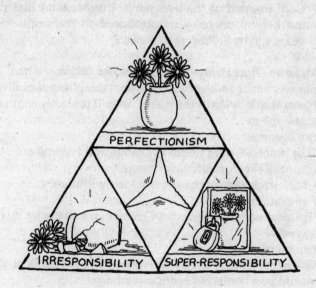

PERFECTIONISM

IRRESPONSIBILITY   SUPER-RESPONSIBILITY

Tips: Solid Responsibility – without Rigid Perfectionism

❏ Keep this – *The Serenity Prayer* – in a handy place:

Grant me the courage to change the things I can change,
the serenity to accept the things I cannot change,
and the wisdom to know the difference.

(This is my secular version. You could use it in its original form
with 'God' inserted at the beginning. I understand that this
wise and helpful prayer was introduced to the world very
many years ago by St Francis of Assisi.)

❏ Make an effort always to *replace 'victim' language* with
phrases which indicate that you are taking responsibility.
For example, 'What's the point? They'll probably continue
to use me to ...'
can become:
'The point is I want things to change and I can take
responsibility for initiating change.'

❏ Check irrelevant *martyr responses* in their infancy.
For example:
'If I clear up this mess, who's going to thank me for it
anyway?'
can become:
'It's in my interest to have this office tidy. A "thank you"
would be a bonus but is not essential.'

❏ Accept the fact that because others may have caused the
problem and continue to be irresponsible, that does not
automatically rob you of *your choice to act responsibly*.
For example:
'Why should I be the one to sort this out? They caused the
problem in the first place and they don't seem to care' (An
automatic reaction from the child part of you.)
can become:

'It is in my interest to do something about this problem, so I am freely choosing to take responsible action.' (The adult part of you taking control.)

❑ *Avoid overdosing on media models* of ridiculous perfection (for example, if you are trying to lose a mere half a stone, don't keep buying magazines whose models are all three stone lighter than you need to be).

❑ Give your *perfectionism a constructive outlet*, but one which isn't going to have a big controlling influence on the shape of your life (perhaps a hobby; arranging the staff social; scrubbing the kitchen floor; cleaning out the car; etc.).

❑ Declare your 'problem' to *friends and colleagues* and ask them to let you know if they see you straying out of the middle section of the responsibility triangle (such as when you are letting others down; when you are being too fastidious; when you are assuming responsibility that is not rightly your own).

Instant Exercise:
Solid Responsibility –
without Rigid Perfectionism

1 Note three things in your life for which you wish to assume responsibility. Think about where you would place yourself in the triangle below in relation to each. If you are not happy with these positions, reflect for a moment on what you could do to change things.

2 Ask yourself if there are any areas in your life where you have a tendency to assume more responsibility than is appropriate. If so, to whom (or which machine!) could you pass on some of that responsibility, and how could you achieve the handover?

The price of greatness is responsibility.

WINSTON CHURCHILL

Driver 13

Calm Concentration –
without Repressed Creativity

(Notebook page 222)

> *It's not enough to be industrious: so are the ants. What are you industrious about?*
>
> HENRY DAVID THOREAU

 There is still a belief in the myth that an ability to concentrate calmly on whatever you want to do is a sign of true motivation. Oh how I wish it were true!

One of the great frustrations about being me is that the more exciting and alluring my goals are, the more difficult it is to summon up the necessary concentration I need to achieve them.

I have found this truth about myself particularly hard to accept because somewhere in my subconscious lurks a belief that a person's ability to concentrate is an indication of his or her level of *'true'* motivation. When, therefore, I find my progress on a project being blocked by my flitting mind and fidgety body, I begin to berate myself with self-talk such as:

> 'If you really wanted to achieve this, you wouldn't be thinking of anything else.'
> 'If this project mattered that much to you, of course you would get down to it more easily.'

I know that this is a dangerously rocky point for my motivation because in the past I have given up the pursuit of many desirable goals because I believed this nonsense. I now know that my inability to concentrate on a task can be caused by many factors such as stress, lack of skill or even over-excitement.

The skill of this Driver is to know how to deal constructively with blocks to concentration without snuffing out the fire of your enthusiasm. The secret is to make sure that you have free access to *both sides of your brain*. We need the logical, analytical left side to execute our action plans with calm concentration, and our emotional right side to help retain our excitement and come up with new creative ideas.

How each of us best achieves this blissful clear-headed but still energized state will depend on our individual personality. I know that within my own family we are all very different on this score. Just recently we have been through a period in our household when we have all had very important exams or deadlines to meet. Some of us had to be quiet, others needed music; some needed to stay only in one room, others had to move around all the time; some of us needed to talk to each other regularly, others became reclusive; some wanted endless coffee, others had to cut out caffeine; some of us needed to scream out their frustration while others quietly bit their nails or scratched their head; some of us needed tidiness, others thrived on clutter.

In the process of each of us reaching our individual states of serenity, you can imagine the 'happy family' scenes we had at times! But as we were all successful in achieving what we wanted, it was certainly worth the struggle.

So, while acknowledging that one secret to developing this Driver might be not to listen to anybody else's 'good advice', I still decided that there were perhaps some general rules and strategies which you might find useful.

Ideally, there are three areas which you will need to check over in order to achieve high-quality concentration without losing your creative abilities:

1 **Your body:** this must be free of tension, but in an energized rather than a deeply relaxed state. It must be being fed

with the best fuel for its particular 'engine' to keep it in this state.

2 **Your mind:** this must be clear and peaceful but lively. It should feel well under your control. It should not, of its own accord, be 'racing', 'flitting', 'getting stuck' or 'going blank'.

3 **Your environment**: this should be appropriately conducive to achieving maximum concentration. It should be tailored to suit your *personal* needs and not jar with your mood or the project you are currently engaged on.

The good news is that if we work hard on the first two areas, we can often function well enough without the third being absolutely perfect. In other words, if we can learn to take our mind and body into the required state of calmness we should be able to concentrate and have access to our creativity *almost* anywhere.

The bad news is that, usually, we have only ourselves to blame if we find we are not 'getting on with it'!

I had to learn this lesson fast when five years ago I moved from Yorkshire to the south of England. In our big (more affordable) house in Yorkshire, I had converted the cellar into a highly conducive working environment in which to write and to see clients. I had chosen compatible calm colours, furnishings and pictures. I had space to move around in and easy access to all my handouts and books. My clients had a welcoming waiting and refreshment area. The location meant that I could rely on almost uninterrupted peace and privacy.

When we moved to Winchester, I had to learn to work in cramped, dual purpose, ill-equipped rooms in my home and also in the austere training rooms of various hotels. Initially I moaned and I moaned until I bored myself (not to mention many others) silly. Eventually, I accepted what I had and was determined to do the work I wanted to do in spite of it. I found that, as a result, I quickly developed a new skill – that of *being able to create the 'right atmosphere' wherever I happen to be working*. My powers of concentration have undoubtedly improved and the whole lesson has been very freeing. I have realized that the *ideal working environment* (which, incidentally, I do now have when I am working in our farmhouse in Spain!) *is a luxury, not a necessity.*

 # Tips: Calm Concentration – without Repressed Creativity

❏ Whenever you hear yourself blaming your cramped office, noisy neighbours, low-flying jets, ticking clocks, untidy kitchen, etc. for your lack of concentration, consciously *turn your focus inwards* and work positively on getting yourself into the right state in both your mind and your body. Remind yourself that you can work on getting a better environment later and that it is a 'bonus' rather than an essential condition for achieving concentration.

❏ When your concentration wanders, *resist self-put-downs and 'kicks' into action*, as well as blame, and *stop*. According to what you need, use your energy to work on releasing your body's physical tension, freeing your mind, or energizing either body or mind.

❏ Get to know what your *best attention span* is. Research would indicate that it is likely to be around 20 minutes, but I know mine varies with the time of day. Remember that it is usually shorter than you'd like to think. As self-motivated people are more workaholic than most, you should probably err on giving yourself a greater number of breaks than you think you'll need, rather than fewer.

❏ Get to know what is *your best time of day* for achieving quiet concentration. Remember how in Driver 10 we looked at how you need different levels of energy for different tasks, so certain times of day are better for some high-energy tasks than others. Similarly, some tasks require more calm concentration than others, so organize your work schedule accordingly.

❏ Appreciate that some tasks, particularly creative ones, need a *'warm-up period'* before you can achieve concentration. I found this fact difficult to accept when I first started writing professionally. As a result, I always underestimated the time I would need and, because I hadn't made allowance for the non-productive first hour or so, I would soon work myself up into a high state of anxiety where concentration became not just difficult but impossible.

❏ Make up your own *'Concentration Kit-bag'*. It can take the form of anything that might help you to retrieve your calmness if it starts to leave you. Here are a few examples:

- personal stereo cassette player with soothing music or sounds of the sea
- picture of your favourite calming scene, person or animal
- a Mandala card for instant meditation
- good quality ear-plugs
- eye-shades or cooling eye-masks
- an aromatherapy candle and matches
- soothing sweets to suck
- small book of reassuring quotations (one of Eileen Campbell's small books, listed in Section 4, would be ideal).
- a symbolic reminder of something you have achieved in the past while in a state of calm concentration

Keep this 'kit-bag' in your desk and don't forget to take it with you whenever you might need it.

Instant Exercise: Calm Concentration – without Repressed Creativity

1 Put down this book now and take your mind and body into a calm state for five minutes. Try my favourite trick for quickly achieving this state.

Lie down with your eyes shielded (or sit in a supported tension-free position with your eyes closed). Take three deep slow breaths and count backwards from 50. As soon as your mind begins to wander, return to 50 until you can reach the number one without stopping.
  Bring a calming image into your mind's eye (e.g. your scene, animal or person) and just focus on it for another minute.

Driver 14

Systematic Organization – without Obtuse Obsessionality

(Notebook page 222)
This is another of my most difficult drivers. Like very many other people I know, I tend to swing between the two extremes of over-organization and total disorganization. But, unfortunately, the swing is not as even or as controlled as I would like it to be.

Deep within me there is a strong *emotional pull towards disorganization*. The guilty strings are being tugged by a stubborn foot-stamping rebel who resists any attempt to maintain systematic order in my life. I am sure it must chuckle with glee when chaos starts to overtake my diary, desk and kitchen, and it hears me coming up with weak excuses such as:

'I haven't had the time ...'

'There are so many more important things to do.'

'Creative people have to be disorganized.'

'With my job I should have a full-time secretary.'

The rational adult part of me actually loves being well-organized. No one has ever had to convince me of the benefits of good order – they have always seemed so obvious. I even enjoy the process of organizing and I take pleasure in knowing that I am extremely competent at it.

So why do I so often behave so 'crazily'? The clue lies in the *feelings of naughtiness* which often accompany my chaos. Underneath the polished exterior of the 'professional me', my inner child is rebelliously digging her heels in and saying:

'Go on, you'll have to make me do it...but I won't make it easy for you.'

Between 5 and 13 years old, I was in a series of understaffed and authoritarian institutions. My daily life was highly regimented and tidiness was considered not just next to godliness, it *was* godliness.

Being a 'saint-in-training', I adopted the routines and rules obsessionally and would willingly encourage everyone else around me to do similarly. Even when we were sent out to play, I would organize games and plan events. At school, I was decorated with good conduct badges, and at guides I was even awarded certificates for tidy camping! When lights went out at night, I didn't give up. I started a secret society complete with its own strict rules, rituals and uniform. (The trappings are probably still under the floorboards of that Children's Home.)

Perhaps if my rebel child had had some room to breathe, then it might not be so disruptive in my subconscious today. But it didn't. Instead, and as a positive result, I acquired some highly useful organizational abilities and a 'fighter' side of me which will not allow itself to be beaten by a stubborn inner child! I have therefore persisted in learning how to manage the latter. I do this by keeping *severely restrained when I'm working, but giving my inner child plenty of 'top-dog' status when I am at play*.

Through my work, I know that many other people struggle with similar problems. Some tell me that their swing is more heavily weighted towards the obsessional side. They find that their over-organization gets in the way of their productivity and creativity. They wish that they could loosen their own reins and not get so anxious and upset when other people (such as spontaneous children and forgetful colleagues) disrupt their organizing habits. So while I am wishing that I could keep myself more in line, they are seeking release from their over-orderly conduct!

But it is important to remember that successful self-motivation does not necessarily require us to steer a middle course. The degree of organization we need will depend on the demands of each specific task. What is certain is that *we must be able to draw upon order when we need it and be able to loosen its restraints when we do not*. To achieve this flexibility some of you may also have to tackle subconscious battles between

'obsessive saints' and your 'unruly devils', but others may simply need to improve and practise your organizational skills. So use whichever of the following tips are appropriate for you.

Tips: Systematic Organization – without Obtuse Obsessionality

❏ Read books (*see Section 4*) and get ideas from other people, but *experiment*, and experiment, until you find the kind of organizational system that suits *you and your needs*. Once you have it in place, stop looking over your shoulder and just get on with it.
❏ To beat boredom or a tendency for obsessionality and other self-sabotaging habits, *change your system frequently*. Having (yet another!) new idea of *my own* is often the best way to trick my rebel within and re-motivate myself to get out of chaos.

❑ Compose and frequently use *positive affirmations* to convince your subconscious that you enjoy being organized. (For example: 'I am proud of my organizational skills. I am tidy because *I* want to be tidy and it is helping me to achieve...')

❑ Find a way of linking your organizational activities to your *vision*. (For example: Put your mission statement or appropriate motivational quotes on your files or filing cabinet.)

❑ Use new *'toys'* to help inspire you. I have often found that a trip around a 'trendy' office stationer's shop to buy myself a treat of a few cheap non-essential items can work wonders.

❑ Devise your own *personal 'to do' lists* and get them photocopied. You could have one for daily use and one for weekly use – different coloured paper for each. Make them look even more professional by getting them typed up before you photocopy them.

Below are some examples that people from one of my groups now use. As they have different lifestyles and needs, their outlines are very different.

Example 1

To Do List   DATE:

•	✔	WORK	•	✔	PERSONAL
		DO:	•	✔	DO:
•		Invoice to TIDB Lett. to D.W.			Exercises
		RING:			RING:
		G. S. BBC			Dentist
		BUY:			BUY:
		Paper clips Fax roll			toothpaste

Example 2

To Do List   Date:

	Do	Ring	Buy
Work	Film Talk to DR Agenda	Bob C. Ginnie	Diary
Home		Sue re. curtains	Milk loo roll
Children	Collect Simon horseriding	Doc.	cough medicine
Course	Finish essay		
Charity Committee	Minutes	B.D. to chat dates	

❑ Take yourself on a *time-management or business studies course*, even if you think you know it all. The presence of others and preaching your wisdom to them can be inspirational. I can assure you that my own organization is bound to take a dramatic up-turn after writing this section!

❑ *Lump boring tasks together* and get them over with in one big sort-out. Make them (e.g. filing and writing out the cheques?) less horrendous by listening to music you enjoy or by giving yourself a treat at the end. (As I edit this text for the 'nth' time I am listening to a wonderful new calming CD!)

❑ Give yourself plenty of opportunity to be *totally disorganized* sometimes. Give yourself a break when you will be *organized by others* from time to time.

Instant Exercise: Systematic Organization – without Obtuse Obsessionality

1 Think of one area of your life or work which could do with some re-organization.

2 Think of one area which could do with a little loosening up in terms of order and ritual.

3 Set yourself a goal for either or both.

4 Review your progress after a time, and reward yourself for having achieved more/less organization, as appropriate.

Driver 15

Meticulous Planning – without Stubborn Inflexibility

(Notebook page 223)
As we have noted several times before, self-motivated people are not willing to let chance play a ruling hand in their lives. However much luck they may meet, they still want to retain overall control of the driving seat. One of the ways that they ensure that they maintain their position is through meticulous planning.

Like so many of these Personality Drivers, planning is not an activity that appears to come naturally to me, and I also seem to have acquired a resistance to it. Somewhere rooted in my belief system is a crazy idea that the 'best' people in life manage to achieve success without plans. For example, this part of me seems to believe that:

– The most articulate speakers talk 'off the cuff'.
– The most artistic artists paint spontaneously.
– The most successful business people just 'have an eye' for a bargain.
– The most proficient gardeners naturally have 'green fingers'.
– The most caring therapists just follow their hearts.
– The greatest tennis champions are simply geniuses with winning streaks.
– The most talented writers are guided by the mysterious muses.

This part of me certainly thinks that a 'real' expert on self-motivation would not have needed to spend months working out the content and format of this book. It 'knows' that if I were truly erudite, words would have flowed flawlessly from my mind to the page. It regards daily word targets and chapter outlines as the food of uninspired 'hacks', and deems them non-essential restrictions for authors from the premier class.

What's so awful about this particular pocket of nonsense in my psyche is that I don't think I can even pass on the blame for it to my deprived childhood or subliminal advertising!

Fortunately, as someone who has actually studied the real-life habits of high achievers, I also have some wiser information in my head. I know that *behind the vast majority of successes in all fields, we are likely to find a well-laid plan*. I also know that, although there are some notable exceptions (e.g. when I am working intuitively as a psychodramatist, and my duty is to follow my client's needs, not my plan!), none of my major achievements would have been possible without my 'plan-before-you-act' rule.

Comprehensive planning not only improves our work projects, it can also underpin effort in many different areas of our lives. I know it has helped me not just to write better books and run a more professional consultancy, but also to be a better parent, homemaker and spouse. I now routinely plan because I know that it will give me the following four advantages:

1 control
2 speed
3 economy
4 moral support

Let me explain these advantages further.

Control

If we do not have a plan for whatever project we are doing, without even knowing it we may be abdicating control to either:

– the *life-script* laid down for us by our early conditioning and our previous experiences of life (for example, in my own life having firm schedules has enabled me to control the effect of my father's role-modelled 'message' about the importance of finishing one task before starting another), or

– *other people* who may use us for the advancement of their plans (isn't it much more difficult to give into yet another request for overtime when we haven't any other activity planned for that evening?).

Speed

Although it often seems quicker at the outset to get straight into working on a project without a plan, once we get going our progress is likely to be much slower. For example, with a plan we can make decisions more easily, have our tools and resources more readily to hand, and arrange our activities so that one flows more naturally and continuously into the next.

We can also often save ourselves time by starting a subsequent task while still completing another. A simple example would be writing a letter to one of next year's prospective customers, while sitting in the waiting room of a current client. Another might be learning the language of a country where you plan to live (or just visit) in five years' time.

Economy

Not only can planning save us time, it can save us money and other resources. The environmentalists are currently making very praiseworthy attempts to make the whole world think ahead so that we can make plans to conserve and recycle natural resources to ensure that the next generation has sufficient to meet their projected needs. Another example, which rings uncomfortable bells for me, might be in the area of home catering. A cook who plans a few meals ahead can save left-overs in the certainty that they will be used and not left to rot in the back of the fridge!

Support

My plans in themselves have often given me an emergency shot of motivation. When I have hit a stumbling block and am feeling like giving up, if I look at the difficulty in the context of my overall plan, it often seems much less significant and I can see how to proceed forward in spite of it. A good example of this advantage in action would be when I meet an attack of writer's block. If I can stop myself from 'trying yet again' to start the new chapter and, instead, return to read through my synopsis, I often become re-inspired with enthusiasm and find I can write again. I am sure that one of the reasons why this happens is that, in the context of the overall plan for the book, finding the *perfect* wording first time round of the opening sentences of just one chapter no longer seems so imperative. Plans can support us by helping us to keep a sense of perspective.

 # Tips: Meticulous Planning – without Stubborn Inflexibility

❑ Allow *more time* than you think you can spare on planning.
❑ Use techniques to stimulate your *creative thinking* (such as brainstorming and mind-mapping) before starting to structure your plan. (To find out more about these techniques, *see page 3* and the books *The Positive Woman* and *Make the Most of Your Mind* listed in Section 4.)
❑ Do a full *outline first* and resist the temptation to go into any detail until this is complete.
❑ Put your major *headings or stages on separate pieces of paper* and then brainstorm, in any order, the details on to each. When I was planning this book, I lived for nearly a week with 50 pieces of paper scattered over the floor in my large room in Spain, and I walked among them jotting down notes on each as they came into my head. Admittedly, this was an opportunity for deluxe planning, but I do use the same basic method for all sorts of

different projects. Sometimes, when I'm on my way to do a last-minute interview, I have to make do with torn up scraps of paper on the seat next to me in the train!

❑ When you're reviewing your brainstormed ideas, use some coloured pens to *highlight* different kinds of action or priority areas. Use symbols (stars, smiling faces, hearts, pointing fingers, etc.) if you feel artistic. Making your work look colourful and eye-catching at this stage is very inspiring.

❑ Make your *final plan look neat* and well-ordered. (I usually need mine to be typed to achieve this state!) Giving your plan a professional finish is motivational, not just at the start but throughout your project.

❑ With each plan you make (however small and boring the task seems), try to relate it to your long-term future *vision and goals*. (For example, planning a new office layout in relation to a commitment to making a contribution to world safety.)

❑ Remember, *very few tasks are too small* for planning.

❑ Remember, even *personal relationships* can benefit from some forethought (planning your and your partner's time off together; planning what you want to say before you make a difficult request, etc.).

❑ Talk through your plan with people who can and will give you *constructive feedback* – but only do so if you are genuinely prepared to adapt it in some way.

❑ Always use *specific dates*, when appropriate, in your plans (rather than 'soon' and 'later'!) and constantly review these, especially when your circumstances (or you) are changing.

Instant Exercise:
Meticulous Planning –
without Stubborn Inflexibility

1 Select an idea for an action project you have in your head, and devise a practice plan in your head. (You do not have to use it.)
2 Imagine that you have been asked to do a *five*-minute talk on one of your pet subjects, and devise an outline plan.

A goal a day keeps the future okay.

DINA GLOUBERMAN

Sharp Decisiveness – without Blindness to Consequence

(Notebook page 223)

> It is in your moments of decision-making that your destiny is
> shaped.
>
> ANTHONY ROBBINS

 The lives of self-motivators are constantly pep-
pered with decision-making. One of the reasons
why they are so good at this important task is
simply that they've had an above-average amount
of practice.

Decisiveness is simply *a social skill masquerading as a personal
quality!* I believe that it can be learned by anyone who has:

1   sound self-esteem
2   consistent courage

As we have already looked at ways in which both these qualities can be built and boosted (Drivers 5 and 9), none of us has
an excuse to be indecisive ever again!

Nearly all the people who come to see me professionally has
to some extent or other lost confidence in their ability to make
at least one decision. They may come because they want *ME* to
decide whether they should:

– ask for a promotion
– change career
– leave their partner

– stand up to their mother
– let their children watch TV

But most of them are much too clever to ask me outright a 'Should I or shouldn't I?' question. They are, after all, often highly intelligent, competent people who have specially select-ed my approach because of its self-help aspects. Decisiveness is a quality which they admire and they often hate to admit that it is a problem for them.

I understand their dilemma so well, because I get so angry and irritated with myself when a spell of it hits me. I long for someone to make my decisions for me. I too start then seeking opinions from all and sundry, and if I do fall into the trap of let-ting others do my deciding, I am rarely satisfied. I end up feel-ing let-down by them as well as myself.

When a persistent attack hits, the answer is rarely as obvious as it seems. I often hear people advise 'a strong arm':

'Just give yourself a deadline and *force* yourself to decide – don't leave the office/room until you have.'

When this apparently easy technique fails, I then hear:

'For goodness sake, just toss a coin.'

or

'Right, if you won't decide I'll decide for you.'

While these solutions may get you out of the occasional dip in decisiveness, they certainly do nothing for persistent attacks – in fact they make them worse.

The best answer, in my experience, is to *give yourself a break* from decision-making and focus on other factors which may be contributing to your basic indecisive state. When, therefore, someone contracts to see me for a series of sessions with this kind of problem, one of the first things I do is ask him or her to make a commitment to making as few decisions as possible until we have reached a certain stage. (This is usually a three-month period.) This is much more difficult to do than it sounds because, by this stage, worrying about 'the decision' has become an obsessional habit. But if they can summon up the courage to *decide not to decide*, they are well rewarded! They get a boost of empowering positive energy and actually begin to believe that there might be a light at the end of their tunnel.

Commonly, I find that the main underlying causes of difficulties with decision-making are:

- **confused values**
  - The block here is not knowing what is the ethically right thing to do. Of course there will always be some decisions which will take us into morally murky waters, but this should never be happening consistently. If we set aside regular times to review and reaffirm our values, our decision-making automatically becomes less stressful and very much quicker.
- **unclear long-term goals**
  - Being able to relate each specific small decision to a bigger objective and our overall mission in life speeds up our choice of alternatives, especially when they all feel equally attractive or awful in the short term.
- **fear of mistakes**
  - Most difficult decisions involve some element of risk. Sometimes they involve taking a chance on getting hurt financially; at other times the risk may be an emotional one. One of the most common fears among even the most outwardly brash people is that of 'looking stupid' if the decision turns out to be a mistake.
- **poor technique**
  - Some people, I find, have just never been taught adequate methods for researching and analysing the pros and cons of different options. Equally, they may never have learned how to access their creativity to enable them to develop these skills. As a result they have a habit of using far less sound approaches, often based on their current mood or some favourite gambling tip.
- **lack of practice**
  - Decision-making is a skill which needs to be used consistently to keep it in tip-top form. I am reminded of this every time I return from a holiday during which I have habitually (and willingly!) handed over decision-making to others.

In Section 4 of this book there are listed several books which are particularly good on this subject (such as those by Anthony Robbins and Roger Dawson), but in the meantime here are some tips based on my own experience.

Tips:
Sharp Decisiveness – without Blindness to Consequence

❏ Try the deadline approach first, but *set a limit on how many deadlines* you are allowed to break before tackling your difficulty from another angle.

❏ Accept that decision-making is a stressful process, but don't be tempted to make a premature decision just to 'get it over with'. Instead, focus on looking at ways of *looking after yourself* while you are under pressure (*see Drivers 10 and 31*).

❏ Remember that the best decisions are rarely made when our system is tanked up to the brim with adrenalin – so an *over-excited state needs as much attention as a state of worry*. (Work on Driver 22 to keep you cool!)

❏ Boost your belief in your ability by *recalling good decisions* you have made. If your mind keeps returning to the bad memories, just jot down what you learned from those wrong decisions, and return to dwelling on the benefits you have gained from the others.

❏ Use both your *right- and left-brain* thinking power for most decisions (that is, stimulate your creative thinking with brainstorms and mind-maps and then use analytical methods to research and sort priorities, etc.).

❏ Regularly *review your values* (*see Driver 8*), because these are often being changed without your conscious consent (such as through advertising and the media). Unconscious modifications can clash with your conscious objectives and undermine your decision-making.

❑ Use contingency planning (*see Driver 15*) to help you cope with your fear of making a mistake.
❑ When you notice yourself worrying *inappropriately* about the opinion of others, don't give yourself a put-down, give yourself a treat!
❑ Make a small poster (or have a T-shirt printed up!) with these words or similar:
'A decision a day will keep worry away.'
– and then practise what you preach!

Confident decision-making is an attainable goal which simply requires practice...there is no magic involved in making good decisions.

ROGER DAWSON

 # Instant Exercise: Sharp Decisiveness – without Blindness to Consequence

1 You are going to practise making a decision right now. You will need several sheets of paper, a pencil and a rubber. (You can reserve your right to change your mind at a later date, but if you follow these steps carefully it is likely that you will want to stick with this decision.)
2 If possible, think of a *real* decision which you are currently struggling with, though alternatively you could choose a hypothetical one which you fear you may have difficulty with in the future. (Remember that in order to improve you will need to choose one which feels a bit difficult, but not too difficult.)
3 Brainstorm (*see page 92*) all the different issues which are involved in this decision (money, health, self-esteem, job prospects, pleasing yourself, pleasing others...etc.)
4 Divide another piece of paper into four columns and in the first column list these issues – sifting out the ones which are least important.

5   In column two, enter a grading for each (perhaps on a
    scale of 1 to 10) according to its *current* importance to
    you in terms of your needs. (Be honest!)
6   In the next column, grade them according to their
    'feel-good' factor. In others words, it is your heart not
    your head which is judge now.
7   In the fourth column, enter a grading which is relevant
    to your long-term objectives and bigger life goals.
8   Now repeat all the above steps with the choices you
    have available.
9   Compare and reflect on the sets of grades and make
    your decision.
10 Devise a contingency plan to use in the unlikely event
    of having made the wrong decision.
    – and now celebrate!

*In every success story, you find someone who has made a coura-
geous decision.*

PETER DRUCKER

Driver 17

Slick Self-presentation –
without Enslavement to Fashion

(Notebook page 224)

> *Successful people are constantly aware of how they are being perceived – and adjust their actions to control their effect...you have only seconds to make a favourable impression and that's all you need.*

D. A. BENTON

 First, I must get my confession over with. This Driver is one on which I have comparatively little expert knowledge. But I was very keen to include it because, although it may not seem obviously relevant to self-motivation, I personally have found self-presentation to be very important.

Recently, in order to clarify my own ideas on the subject I have had many discussions with image-consultants and designers. The diagram overleaf summarizes my conclusions.

Of course I am not alone in having recently realized the importance of image. Consultancies in this field have become a booming business over the last few years. I have welcomed this growth partly because it pleases my aesthetic eye and partly because it has provided many useful 'tools' and tips for people who lack self-confidence. But I have also found myself feeling some concern as I have observed its disempowering effect on some people.

Many self-motivated people are seeking help in this area because they know that the right image can enhance their chances of success. Unfortunately, when confronted with a

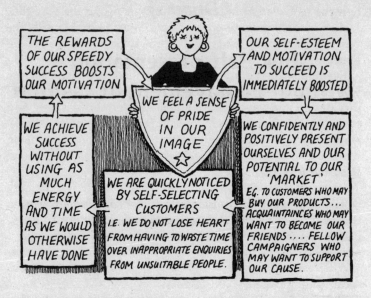

THE REWARDS OF OUR SPEEDY SUCCESS BOOSTS OUR MOTIVATION

OUR SELF-ESTEEM AND MOTIVATION TO SUCCEED IS IMMEDIATELY BOOSTED

WE FEEL A SENSE OF PRIDE IN OUR IMAGE

WE ACHIEVE SUCCESS WITHOUT USING AS MUCH ENERGY AND TIME AS WE WOULD OTHERWISE HAVE DONE

WE ARE QUICKLY NOTICED BY SELF-SELECTING CUSTOMERS I.E. WE DO NOT LOSE HEART FROM HAVING TO WASTE TIME OVER INAPPROPRIATE ENQUIRIES FROM UNSUITABLE PEOPLE.

WE CONFIDENTLY AND POSITIVELY PRESENT OURSELVES AND OUR POTENTIAL TO OUR 'MARKET' E.G. TO CUSTOMERS WHO MAY BUY OUR PRODUCTS... ACQUAINTAINCES WHO MAY WANT TO BECOME OUR FRIENDS .... FELLOW CAMPAIGNERS WHO MAY WANT TO SUPPORT OUR CAUSE.

super-smart image consultant, some instantly develop an urge to become his or her clone! Their thirst for individual expression becomes submerged beneath a desperate desire to become an up-to-the-minute, up-market colour-coordinated charmer!

Of course, a skilled, reputable consultant will battle through this inappropriate fawning. The best make it their business to help each customer create his or her own personal style – but some insecure, arrogant or unscrupulous ones certainly do not. This is true too in other related fields of self-presentation such as the design of products, leaflets, logos and almost anything else with which many people working today happen to be closely associated.

A few years ago I went through a phase of not being able to find the 'right' presentation style for my programmes and brochures. I tried a multitude of designs and designers. Each time a new set of leaflets and paper came to my office I felt despairing. Even though it was difficult to fault many on their eye-catching designs, I knew they were 'wrong' and it was very hard to find enough enthusiasm to send them out.

Sometimes I even found myself apologizing for the way they looked before I gave them to people to read – not exactly the best first impression to set as someone selling courses in confidence and positive action!

Eventually the penny dropped. I realized that the problem was not the quality of the designs. I happen to like contemporary design and have always taken an interest in fashion, and several of the designs were appealing in this respect. At last I realized that the problem was that they did not present an *accurate non-verbal message about my personality, philosophy and method of working*.

I then decided to try a designer, Jan Hildebrand, who usually worked in very different fields to my own but who knew me well and happened to have personal experience of my work. Instead of telling her the kind of design I wanted, my only brief was that the *style and colours should reflect me and the way I work*.

When Jan produced her designs they immediately felt right because they felt like 'me'. At last, I knew I had the correct 'tools' to enable me to create that all-important first and lasting impression; I distributed my new leaflets and cards with pride and enthusiasm.

If this is a Driver which also needs a bit of attention on your part, these tips from an amateur in the field may help.

Tips: Slick Self-presentation – without Enslavement to Fashion

❏ Never sell out on your *individuality* – to refresh your mind about what it is that makes you unique, use the tips in Drivers 20 and 21.

❏ Unless you are in the art business, don't let your own *'artiness'* play a dominant deciding role in your choice of style.

❏ Maintain control over the *fashion-victim* part of you. Keep it happy with 'frill' purchases and don't let it make major decisions.

❏ Don't penny pinch on presentation – be prepared to *spend as much you can afford*. This is rarely good ground for bargain-hunting. Remember – a high-class look will give you high-class feelings (and results!).

❏ Select designers and image consultants who *listen* first and advise second.

❏ Remember, a *clean and polish* can sometimes give us as a good a 'buzz' as an expensive change.

❏ Keep trying until you find a style which *YOU like* and which inspires you.

Instant Exercise:
Slick Self-presentation –
without Enslavement to Fashion

1 Select *three* (and only three!) adjectives which sum up the main message you want to present about yourself and your work or products.

2 Ask yourself if the way you are dressed now is in tune with these adjectives.

3 Ask yourself whether the presentation of your last piece of work was in tune with these.

4 If either of your answers to 2 or 3 were 'No' or 'I think so,' resolve now to make your presentation reflect you and your strengths.

Driver 18

Positive Problem-solving –
without Immunity to Despair

(Notebook page 224)

*The best thing about the future is that it only comes one day at
a time.*

ABRAHAM LINCOLN

 Now I am back to being on very sure ground with
this Driver. First, I have a history of thousands and
thousands of solved problems behind me, and secondly, I still have a vivid recollection of what it's
like to feel deep despair!

Indeed, as I begin to write on this subject I am aware that my
own personal life has given me enough material to fill a book,
and that my experiences as a professional could extend it into
an encyclopedia!

So, partly in order to make my task manageable and partly
because I thought it would be a useful memory aide, I have
limited myself to a nine-point strategy and have broken this
down into three sections: the As, Bs, and Cs.

I will now attempt to guide you concisely through the steps.

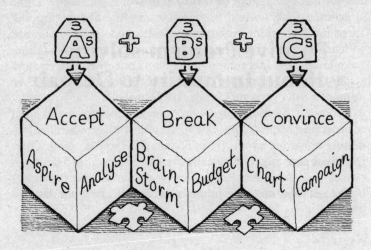

The Three As

ACCEPT

the first crucial step is to *check for any hint of denial* of the problem. Unfortunately, the more serious a problem is the more likely we are to adopt this defensive mode. If we are the 'independent-type' we will be doubly at risk. This is particularly true if we have come from a background which has helped to build us into 'fighters' and 'survivors'.

I am sure that the subject matter of this book will attract many readers who are like this, and who therefore have a tendency to say to themselves:

– 'I don't want to hear about that now – I'll cross that bridge when I come to it' (that is, when the crisis overwhelms you).
– 'I'll ignore it because I'm not going to let a thing (or a person) like that get me down' (that is, not until you are down anyway).

This can be a very dangerous mode to slip into. Once we are set in it our blinkers tend to grow rapidly and we literally cannot see our problem or be aware of how it is escalating. Often concerned relatives and friends ring me to make an appointment for such independently-minded loved ones. I have had to learn to zip up my heart and refuse. Years of experience have taught me that unless the person concerned can demonstrate enough acceptance of his problem to arrange his own appointment, everyone's effort will be wasted.

But on the positive side, when someone does reach the point of accepting responsibility for solving his problem he is immediately rewarded by a wave of instant relief and renewed energy. This phenomenon is usually attributed to some mysterious power that my clients think I must possess. Unfortunately I have to disillusion them quickly and give all the credit back to them!

ASPIRE

Next we have to *set goals* and try to embrace a vision of what we would like to see at the end of the tunnel. At this stage it is unlikely that we will see a solution to the problem, but what we can do is *visualize and feel ourselves in a problem-free state*. For example, an overweight person may not know how she will lose her weight, but it is very motivating to have a clear picture of how life might be different with a fit, healthy, trim physique to depend on. Similarly, a couple going to marriage guidance or companies entering a negotiating process will be more motivated to work through the pain of conflict if at the outset they are fully aware of the rewards that a resolution will bring.

ANALYSE

At this stage the problem is like a jumbled-up jigsaw. If we pull out a bunch of pieces at random and try to begin sorting, we soon feel despair. It's only when we have separated the pieces from their ill-fitting partnerships, laid them individually out on a table and then grouped like with like that we begin to feel we can create order out of chaos.

We need to go through the same process with any baffling problem. We must clarify:

1 the different *aspects* (people/finances/psychological blocks/ poor communication/inadequate resources/faulty organizational structure, etc.)

2 the *links* between these aspects (the psychological blocks which are preventing good communication/mismanagement of finances which is causing inadequacy of resources, etc.)

3 highlight which areas are *our responsibility* and have a chance of being resolved through taking a positive problem-solving approach

4 choose the *priority* areas on which we will first focus our attention.

The Three Bs

BREAK

I can't emphasize the importance of this stage enough because I know that it is one which is so easy to skip. If we do, however, we jeopardize the success of the whole process.

After our careful analysis of a problem, it is important to take a break from it. Our aim in doing this is twofold:

1 to refresh and recharge our *energy*

2 to stimulate our *creativity* (we know that the right brain works best when our body is relaxed and our left, analytical brain is switched off).

Ideally we should not return to the problem until we have reached a stage where we have been able to switch off from it *at least for a full five minutes*. (Bigger and more chronic problems obviously require a longer break period.)

BRAINSTORM

Brainstorming is a way of letting our *creativity have free rein*. We can do this either on our own or with a group of people. If we are doing it on our own, it sometimes helps to allow the different sides of our personality to make their separate contributions (i.e. the peacemaker/the organizer/the miser/ the fighter, etc. within us).

For those of you who are unfamiliar with the technique of brainstorming, these are the simple steps you take:

How to Do a Brainstorm

1 Put a key word or phrase which sums up the issue in the centre of the page. Around it, jot down *any idea* as and when it comes into your head, without judging or analysing it. Sometimes it helps to have your brainstorming sheet of paper around for a few days in a handy place so that you can add words when they hit you unexpectedly (the right brain does not work to order very well!).
2 When the ideas have dried up, cross out those which are obviously *'crazy' or duplicated*.
3 Draw lines and arrows between the ideas which appear to be *linked*.
4 *List* these on another sheet, or make a meaningful diagram of them.
5 *Select one* which you want to explore further and can experiment with immediately.

BUDGET
Now it's reality time! You need to work out clearly:

• what your problem-solving ideas may cost you in terms of *money, materials and time*
• what you already have *currently available* of the above
• the *shortfall* and your plans for meeting it

The Three Cs

CONVINCE
Your work here may fall into two sections. You may need first to convince *yourself* that the problem can be resolved. This is

especially true if the last stage has pushed your despair button, as it usually does for me. Here you can turn to your Driver 3 for a shot of optimism.

Secondly, you may need to *attempt* to convince *other people* (that there is a problem; that it is worth solving or that you, perhaps with their help, are capable of solving it.) It is Driver 27 you will need most help from here.

CHART

This is the planning stage. It is important to formulate a *step-by-step action plan* complete with its specific achievable *goals*, target *dates* and a *review* structure.

If you are working in conjunction with anyone else, it is important that your planning has also *clarified your expectations* of each other in the following areas:

– problem-solving action
– communication of progress
– provision of mutual support

CAMPAIGN

At this stage you have to *stop thinking and start doing*. It is a time when I find that excuses start creeping out of the woodwork in their hundreds. I hear myself saying:

– 'I haven't the time just now.'
– 'I hadn't thought of consulting _____ I must have a meeting with them first.'
– 'There's a new book on the subject; perhaps I ought to read that first.'
– 'I've just remembered that _____ might be offended.'
– 'The sun's shining today, it might rain tomorrow and I can do it then.'
– '…but I should really fix…first and then…!'

If your problem-solving gets sabotaged in this way you'll find working on Driver 24 should help.

This is the stage that reveals the armchair problem-solvers in their true colours. It is one of the best tests of our motivation because it is rarely achieved without the involvement of some discomfort and pain. If these feelings are likely to tip you once again in the direction of despair, don't forget to allow more than *adequate time for self-nurturing and support* (see Driver 31 for tips in this area).

 # Tips: Positive Problem-solving – without Immunity to Despair

❑ Accept that despair is fairly inevitable at the outset of creative problem-solving. An alternative to denying it is to give it some first-class *'wallowing' time* (spend time with friends who can stand your moaning phase because they have faith that it will pass; allow yourself to feel and express your fears and tears, however 'wimpish' you may feel this to be).

❑ Use a selection of *coloured pens* to write or highlight your notes and plans. This will stimulate your right brain and help you to feel positive.

❑ Use *giant sheets of paper* for your brainstorms, especially when you think you only have one or two ideas. You'll be amazed at how soon the space gets filled.

❑ Remember, our *best ideas for solutions often come when we are relaxing*, rather than working, so keep a notebook handy in the bathroom and by your bed or favourite armchair.

❑ Meet in large groups to brainstorm but then select a *small working party* (3 – 4 people) for the rest of the problem-solving stages.

❑ Expect and prepare for *conflict* when working as a team. Conflict can stimulate new ideas and help maintain high energy levels if it is managed well. If you have difficulty in handling conflict or controlling your anger, get some help in this area. You could start by reading my book *Managing Anger* and some of the other titles listed in Section 4.

❏ Before going into a particularly difficult problem-solving group meeting, play a *calming cassette* (such as my *Anger Control Workout* or a positive thinking or relaxation tape).

❏ If you (and/or your colleagues) feel your problem-solving brain is getting rusty or you have lost your enjoyment of these kinds of challenges, re-stimulate this side of yourself with *fun activities* such as puzzles, games, crosswords, treasure hunts, etc.

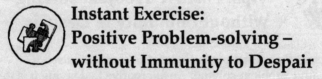

Instant Exercise: Positive Problem-solving – without Immunity to Despair

Review the problems you currently have sitting in the 'pending store' of your mind. Select a minor one which you could work on now, using the A-B-C strategy above.

Reliable Intuition – without Acting on Every Hunch

(Notebook page 225)

I have found that great ideas come when you have a great desire to have them.

CHARLES CHAPLIN

 Would you like the power to bring your heaven down to earth? If so, this is the Driver for you! When intuition is working for us, not only do we *achieve great things*, but we *enjoy achieving them*.

I am sure, like me, you have heard many eminent people talk in the media about this subject. Alongside hard work and courage, intuition is one of the most commonly quoted 'secrets' of success. When interviewed about their extraordinary achievements in their work, sport, hobby, campaign or even marriage, you often hear these kinds of explanations:

'It just felt the right thing to do.'

'I knew instinctively what needed to be done.'

'I just woke up one morning with a quiet realization and...'

'I was out walking and out of the blue I had this blinding flash of insight and ...'

'From the moment I saw her, I had a feeling that this was meant to be.'

'It was just a gut reaction but it was so strong that...'

'I don't know where the idea came from – it just popped into my head and...'

It is commonly believed that such people are 'blessed' with the gift of intuition and others are just not so lucky. But recent research would suggest that anyone with a functioning right brain has this capacity. So *if you are capable of feeling emotion you are equally capable of harnessing this inspiring internal power*.

Maybe you are already aware of this aspect of your potential, but do you use it to its best advantage? If you do you would be unusual. In today's scientific and analytically-minded world, our sixth sense (as intuition is often called) has become relegated to the status of 'weird feelings'. Most people tend to disclose these only to trusted friends and even then, only once they have been *proved* to be correct. Very few people allow intuition any substantial guiding power over their lives.

Personally I am finding that this part of me has become increasingly active and useful over the last ten years. I find I am gaining more and more respect for my hunches, flashes of insight and intuitive responses. I am excited by them because they are generally 'spot-on' in their guidance and save me so much thinking time and energy.

Mystics among you might be quite disappointed to hear that my own explanation of how I developed this faculty is boringly down-to-earth. But fellow pragmatists might be interested (and possibly inspired?) by my mundane understanding of how this happened.

As a result of some searching self-reflection and considerable study of the theories behind such phenomena, I have concluded that there have been four main factors which have contributed towards the development of my own intuitive powers:

– First, because I am a glutton for learning and new experiences, as the years have gone by my brain's memory bank has amassed a rich and *vast store of information*.
– Secondly, as a by-product of my own personal development work (e.g. development of self-trust through self-awareness and emotional control; stress management and creativity training), my *right brain now works much more efficiently*. It can now sort the information in my memory bank much more rapidly into meaningful patterns from which I can draw instant conclusions and predictions.

– Thirdly, I have learned when it is *appropriate to use my right brain and when I should use my left one*, and I know how to switch quickly into either mode.

– Fourthly, my *increased confidence in my ability to cope with any possible failure* has enabled me to take the risk of testing out my intuitive perceptions.

Although I am not able to put these conclusions through rigorous trials to examine their 'truth', they are also supported by observing similar developments in my clients' intuitive powers. I therefore feel confident enough to offer you the following more specific tips on how to strengthen this Driver in you.

Tips: Reliable Intuition – without Acting on Every Hunch

❏ Secretly exercise your intuition by using it to make *instant gut guesses* about people you see in the tedious queues of post offices, trains or airports. Having done this, check out your right brain's efficiency by searching analytically for clues to support your initial guesses – such as in the person's apparel, voice, facial expression or by making conversation with the person. (Your right brain will have chunked together a whole mass of detailed information it has deemed relevant to your guess, that is current observations plus past similar perceptions. Don't forget that, because it is also the keeper of your emotions, it will have selected these in tune with your current mood.)

❏ Read books or watch films which will give you practice in finding *connections between different phenomena* (for example, thrillers and murder mysteries; biographies which attempt to understand their subjects from a psychological, biological and sociological point of view).

❏ Enrol in a *class* which will help you do the above (perhaps one that takes a look at art/TV/films/events, etc. in their total historical, cultural, political or religious contexts).

❏ Watch *comedy* shows whose humour is based on challenging our normal perceptions (for example by using puns, impersonations, staging unlikely meetings between contrasting people, etc.).

❏ Set aside some time to *gaze 'unthinkingly'* at abstract or surrealistic pictures and photo collages (you'll find these in modern art galleries but also in the art section of any good library) and note what feelings and ideas spontaneously emerge.

❏ Play *party games* which call upon your imagination (such as passing a broom around a group and having each person transform it into an imaginary tool for another purpose; charades).

❏ Make a habit of *listening* for and noting down your intuitive response whenever you need to make a decision. (Don't forget that in most circumstances it is advisable to check this against your more logical side before finally deciding.) By keeping this kind of *record*, you will soon learn how much you can trust your intuition.

❏ Give yourself plenty of practice in *switching off your left brain* and allowing your creative, emotional brain to take over (through meditation; listening to emotional music or rhythmic natural sounds such as a rippling brook; doodling; hot baths with sensuous smells in flickering candlelight, etc.).

 # Instant Exercise: Reliable Intuition – without Acting on Every Hunch

1 Think of an occasion on which you have followed a hunch with great success (perhaps a time when you selected a new friend from a crowd of strangers/an unexplored holiday destination/an idea for a new business venture).

2 Think of a hunch which you followed but which turned out not to be so insightful.

3 Compare the two occasions, using your analytical side to note what kind of information your right brain may have collated in order for you to have had these hunches (that is, was it using emotionally-laden past experiences? Had it been influenced by subliminal advertising? Had it picked up diverse clues from a range of experiences?).

The majority of business people are incapable of having an original idea because they cannot free themselves from the restraints of logic.

DAVID OGILVY

Ideas, Ideas, that's what we need.

HELENA RUBENSTEIN

Driver 20

Searching Self-reflection – without Frustrating Self-absorption

(Notebook page 225)

Real greatness consists of being master of yourself.

DANIEL DEFOE

Autobiographies are rarely easy or financially rewarding tasks to set yourself in your golden years. So why do so many successful people want to give themselves this kind of headache when they least need to? Some may have a purely altruistic desire to pass on their wisdom. But I would guess that many others are just seduced by the opportunity to air their lifelong fascination with the workings of themselves!

I am convinced that self-reflection is a key common quality among persistently high achievers. It is one that helps to keep them motivated, interested and active even when they have reached the top.

Over the last five years, I and other colleagues have noticed a sharp increase in the numbers of successful people who are turning to personal development work even though they are not experiencing any particular difficulties. We find that they are people who have always privately thought deeply about themselves and the pattern of their lives, and who are convinced that this habit of self-questioning has been a contributing factor in their success.

They often come initially into our world of psychotherapy

because they are *interested* to find out more about the make-up of their subconscious self and its impact on their lives and relationships. Their appetite might have been whetted by reading an article, hearing a talk or meeting someone who has enthused about his or her own experience.

After satisfying their curiosity about their own psychological history, I notice that many more are choosing to continue to have sessions or attend workshops because they find having *a regular date with introspection highly stimulating*. What is sad is that they often express guilt and misgivings about doing so. Typically, such clients and I have to work through their fear of others perceiving them as neurotic, their guilt about taking up a therapist's time when others could be more needy, and their anxiety about becoming self-obsessed. The breakthrough comes when they can unashamedly allow themselves the luxury of enjoying the experience.

This growing demand for services to aid self-understanding has recently been highlighted and investigated by the media. Quite rightly, as a result of a few disturbing findings professional standards are being scrutinized and we are currently witnessing campaigns to weed out the 'con-artists' and unethical practitioners which every fast-developing industry seems to sprout.

Quite wrongly, however, this 'backlash' movement is now turning its venomous power towards the activity of self-reflection itself. The public are being fed with scare-mongering stories of how it can lead to the kind of self-absorption that breaks up loving families, encourages dependency on anti-social cults and diverts people's energy and resources away from the greater needs of deprived others.

My own experience of people who are committed to ongoing self-reflection is quite the opposite. As a direct result of becoming more self-aware and self-questioning I see them becoming better parents, better friends, better workers and better citizens. Furthermore, self-understanding fires up their motivation because, for example:

– They see their strengths more clearly and realistically and so can use them more appropriately.

– They can concentrate energy on improving particular weaknesses which they see block their progress.

– They have more self-control because they identify unhelpful patterns before these have become entrenched bad habits.

– Their relationships improve as they take more responsibility for their difficulties.

Here endeth my sermon!

– but I hope you are convinced enough to try some of the following tips from an unashamed addict of self-reflection.

Tips: Searching Self-reflection – without Frustrating Self-absorption

❏ Write the following *questions* out on a card, or photocopy this page.

1) What have I enjoyed about today?
2) What have I disliked about today?
3) What have I achieved today?
4) What contribution have I made to others or my environment today?
5) Have I surprised myself in any way today?
6) What would I like to happen tomorrow to make it a satisfying day for me? (Be realistic!)

Set aside a specific period of ten minutes a day for a month to ask yourself these questions. You could use some 'scrap time' in which to do this, such as when you are travelling home from work, taking the dog for a walk, watering the garden, cleaning the kitchen, etc. At the end of the month you should have developed the habit of asking yourself these kinds of questions daily.

❏ Beg, borrow or buy a self-help book with a *programme of*

exercises designed to further your self-understanding
(*see Section 4 for many suggestions*).

❑ Keep checking that your self-reflective activities (self-help
or any other) are still fascinating you. If they become a
chore, don't abandon the task but resolve to *change your
method*. A browse around personal development
bookshelves will show you just how many there are for
developing self-understanding. I am convinced there is at
least one to suit everyone's needs and tastes. Seek advice
from a professional if you still can't make progress or if
you uncover very worrying insights about yourself (they
don't all charge a small fortune!).

❑ Increase your motivation and make your self-reflection
more fun and supportive by joining or forming a small
personal development *group* or an evening class in
humanistic psychology.

❑ Take regular *breaks* to avoid becoming too introspective.
Self-reflection is best done in short regular bursts with
plenty of space in between for putting your insights into
practice. My own groups designed for this purpose meet
once a fortnight or once a month only in 'term-time' – we
have found that this kind spacing works very well.

❑ Mix 'business' with pleasure and treat yourself once a
year to a *retreat or short personal development holiday break*
(such as the courses I run in my centre in Spain, and
others which often advertise in the Activity Holiday
sections in newspapers.)

 Instant Exercise:
Searching Self-reflection –
without Frustrating Self-absorption

Imagine that a film company has been hired to make a film about you. They have been given an unlimited budget and total freedom on its style and on the actors and director to be used. They are just about to approach you for your advice, so note down your spontaneous answers to the following questions:

1 Which type of film would you choose to reflect your own overall style (documentary/blockbuster adventure/ intellectual drama/grand opera/musical/comedy of manners/cartoon, etc.)?
2 Which famous actor or actress would you choose to play you?
3 What would be the title and sub-title of the film?
4 Compose two sentences which summarize the essence of this film and which could be used to market it.

Over the next week or so, think about your instant responses to these questions and re-write your answers if you want to do so.

Later, if you want to, you could share these questions with a friend (choose someone who will take the exercise seriously!) and ask for his or her suggestions. Note how his or her answers differ from your own and discuss why this might be so.

It takes a long time for people to recognize their soul-mates when they have too limited an idea of who they are themselves.

THEODORE ZELDIN

Pride in Individuality – without Disregard for Human Commonality

(*Notebook page 226*)

> *Man is more interesting than men…each is more precious than all.*
>
> ANDRÉ GIDE

 A couple of weeks ago I heard a feature on the radio about eccentricity. It was in response to some research which had revealed that eccentric people score much higher than the average on happiness scores!

Needless to say, this news was music to my ears. Several times already in this book I have revealed how highly I esteem this quality. Much of my work is devoted to helping people recover buried individuality and I am continually excited by the seemingly endless diversity I see in human beings.

But you may also have noted how much of a pragmatist I am as well. I know that a society peopled entirely with unrestrained eccentrics would be unmanageable, unsafe and not very productive. I also know that in a world peopled only with rugged individualists we would lose the companionship, support and stimulation we get from being members of a species and a culture that give us so much in common with each other.

So, given a choice I would not swap the struggle between my love of individuality and need for commonality for the bliss of pure eccentricity. I suspect that most of you reading this book would not either, but what we might have some dis-agreement about is what we would consider an ideal balance between the two. This has to be *finely adjusted not only to suit each person's taste but also to suit our circumstances.*

Unfortunately, fewer and fewer of us seem to be achieving a satisfactory balance. Most people I meet complain that nowadays they have far too little freedom to express their individuality. In order to keep their job or keep the peace of their community they feel compelled to conform to rigidly standardized codes of behaviour, dress, speech, letter writing, child-rearing and many other aspects of daily life. An addi-tional worry I often hear expressed is that as the world devel-ops into more of a global community there will be even less variation in personal style. Already, most major cities in the world have a familiar look and feel about them. We are likely to see many of the same shops, fashions, hairstyles, advertise-ments and styles of building as we know back home.

The short-term gains of allowing our individuality to get depressed in this way are tempting. We can save money, time and angst. Initially we even notice a surge in motivation as we feel at a cozy oneness with each other and our purpose. It's therefore no wonder that so many people relinquish their indi-viduality so readily.

In the long term all these benefits are, of course, negated as the conformity and boredom create apathy, low commitment and resentment. Successfully self-motivated people would never allow this to happen. They know and appreciate too well the value of being able to feel and express their own clear sense of identity.

No bird soars too high if it soars with its own wings.

WILLIAM BLAKE

Tips: Pride in Individuality – without Disregard for Human Commonality

❑ Ask yourself regularly the simple question:
'*Am I being myself?*'

❑ Never make a habit of holding back on your opinions and ideas just because they don't appear to fit in or seemingly cannot be used. *Express* them even if you do decide, or are forced, to 'go along with the majority'.

❑ Use '*I*' *language*, rather than the more alienating third person (such as 'People would say ...' 'Everybody thinks that' 'One would suppose that…').

❑ If you have to wear a *uniform* for your profession, try to find a way of doing your 'own thing' with it. (A bus queue full of school-uniformed teenagers will give you some ideas!)

❑ Keep your *personal work space personal*. Like uniforms, personalizing standard office furniture can be viewed as an interesting challenge!

❑ Remind yourself (and any critics you may encounter) that the people who have contributed most to the common good are often very *individualistic characters*. Albert Schweitzer is just one example, and he practised what he preached.

To work for the common good is the highest creed.
ALBERT SCHWEITZER

❑ Welcome *conflict* as a way of discovering more about your own and others' individuality. See family arguments and heated debates in the office as opportunities to exercise this Driver!

❑ Watch TV *debates* and discuss these with friends.

Instant Exercise: Pride in Individuality – without Disregard for Human Commonality

To exercise your awareness of both your individuality and commonality:

1 Think of today's main news stories and note down six names and a few identifying features about the people who were mentioned or featured (famous or otherwise).
2 Think about what you have in common with each of these people, such as 'I am a woman/have suffered pain/have been a child/do get angry', etc.
3 Think about the factors which differentiate you from each of these people, such as 'I am not politically active/I am much taller/I am more scientifically minded/I haven't any children/I wasn't born during a war', etc.

Never forget that only dead fish swim with the stream.

MALCOLM MUGGERIDGE

Deep Emotionality – without Enslavement to Feelings

(Notebook page 226)

> *To feel deeply motivated, we must feel deep feelings.*

 A banal statement of an obvious truth – but a truth which, particularly in Great Britain, is still very hard for many people to swallow. Small wonder when we have been culturally conditioned to keep so much emotion stuck in the back of our throats!

As a nation we are urged by leaders, managers and teachers to work (or look for work) with passionate enthusiasm. But when we succeed, we are told that it's 'bad form' to jump for joy. And when we fail, we are politely reminded that only babies cry over spilled milk!

Recently, in many 'enlightened' homes and workplaces there is a growing acceptance that this crazy repression of feeling is bad for both mental and physical health. People are being urged to express their feelings anywhere and at any time. As the emotional dams are burst, the inevitable floods of histrionics are causing chaos:

- Children are screaming abuse at tearful parents and quaking teachers.
- Frustrated employees are thumping fists at bewildered bosses.
- Angry customers are threatening obviously bored and resentful shop assistants.
- Envious politicians are publicly cutting each other's throats.

Not surprisingly, people are getting frightened and beginning to yearn nostalgically for the 'good old, genteel' days.

So what is the answer for those of us who want and need to keep the fire alight in our belly? I believe it lies in learning and practising the *skills of emotional effectiveness*. These are personal and social skills which enable us to *feel as deeply as our hearts and senses dictate without the risk of losing control over our behaviour*. Even on a day-to-day basis, we can retain the exhilaration and stimulation of our strong feelings without having to worry that we will become distracted from our purpose. We are able, for example:

- to enjoy a peaceful recharging lunch hour knowing that we can 'psyche ourselves up' for the difficult serious meeting after lunch
- to have passionate arguments with our partner knowing that we will not later 'take it out' on the children or the neighbour's cat
- to feel deeply envious of others' achievements but still behave civilly and fairly with them and use them as inspiring role-models
- to be bitterly disappointed with our progress but retain our determination and not sink into a pit of sabotaging despair
- to sense a pleasurable attraction towards a beautiful colleague while maintaining a professional, friendly relationship with him or her
- to feel wounded by an unfair put-down from a waiter but be able to make a cool assertive complaint and not get indigestion
- to be genuinely concerned about others' distress but continue to work enthusiastically towards our own exciting goals

In summary, emotional effectiveness enables us to trust ourselves enough to be the kind of person we want to be. It is essential for both our self-esteem and the attainment of our goals.

For some people, acquiring sound emotional control can take years of personal development work. (I know because I have had to do it!) But for others it may only require a few weeks of brushing up on strategies and becoming a little more aware. Below I list 11 key areas which I have found useful to focus on when learning the skills of emotional control.

The Eleven Essentials of Emotional Effectiveness

1 **Awareness**
   (a) of yourself – your body and its physiological responses to emotion; personal warning signals of emotional overload; own Achilles' heel
   (b) of other people – developing sensitivity and empathy; understanding and responding appropriately to the body language messages of others
   (c) of your culture – normal codes of behaviour; manners; beliefs; prejudices

2 **Thought control**
   – reframing negative thinking; stimulating your imagination and creativity; quietening racing thoughts with meditation; using positive visualizations to control worry; employing self-hypnosis

3 **Relaxation techniques**
   – methods of bringing your body back to normal physiological functioning; reducing the flow of adrenalin through deep relaxation; yoga

4 **Communication skills**
   – articulateness; active listening; effective presentation; using non-verbal 'language' effectively

5 **Preparation strategies**
   – scripting; problem-solving mnemonics; contingency planning

6 **Behavioural training**
   – role-play; coaching; rehearsing; assertiveness training

7 **Cathartic release**
   – thumping cushions; outlets through sport; ability to have 'a good cry' or a 'good scream'
8 **Constructive channelling**
   – positive outlets for built-up frustration and anger; opportunities to let off steam; opportunities to use nurturing energy appropriately; avoidance of destructive or abusive sexual 'diversions'.
9 **Emotional healing**
   – efficient mourning; dealing with backlog of old emotional wounds; strategies for healing hurt and abuse
10 **Lifestyle management**
   – time-management and organizational skills; developing an ability to manage pressure, transition and change
11 **Relationship skills**
   – how to use people for support; negotiation and conciliation skills; relationship maintenance; starting and ending relationships effectively.

You will find the following tips for controlling specific common emotions useful as 'Quick fixes'. I appreciate that they are far from being a 'cure-all' and you may need to work quite hard to develop some of the skills listed above.

Tips: Deep Emotionality – without Enslavement to Feelings

❏ If you feel *fear*, use relaxation techniques to blot out worrying thoughts with positive affirmations and then *get prepared* to face the challenge behind your fear by using the techniques of rehearsing, visualization, scripting, etc.).
❏ When you feel *hurt*, acknowledge what you have lost (self-esteem, credibility, etc.), express your grief appropriately and set an achievable goal for finding a compensating *replacement*.

❏ When you feel *guilt*, name the standards your subconscious perceives you have violated; check that these are your own (and not unknowingly acquired from others); assess whether they are currently relevant; if you still feel guilty, vow to make recompense.

❏ When you feel *frustration*, acknowledge this as a sign that you could be doing better; release your tension and then try a *new approach*.

❏ When you feel *disappointment*, acknowledge you have been let down and review and re-state your *goals and expectations*.

❏ If you feel *inadequate*, accept that your skills and knowledge are not 'up to the job', then write an action plan for learning or refreshing them.

❏ If you feel *angry*, accept that you are probably in an irrational thinking mode; stop and get some distance from the person or situation; release your physical tensions safely; breathe slowly and then prepare a script to help you assertively express your feelings and/or needs.

❏ When you feel *loneliness*, accept that you either need more *connection with people* or that your *self-esteem* is low. Test out which is the cause by immediately giving yourself more of one or the other.

❏ If you feel *over-excited*, accept that you need *more outlets, challenge or fun* in your life on a regular basis; calm yourself down by controlling your breathing pattern; meditate and then think of ways to build more of these experiences into your lifestyle.

Instant Exercise: Deep Emotionality – without Enslavement to Feelings

1 List all the emotions you have either fully experienced or suppressed during the last week.
2 Re-read the 11 essentials above and assess what skills you may need to develop to become more emotionally effective.

Self-trust is the first secret of success.

RALPH WALDO EMERSON

Driver 23

Stringent Self-criticism – without Suffocating Self-abuse

(Notebook page 227)

Some people spend their lives failing and never notice.

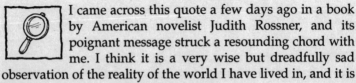 I came across this quote a few days ago in a book by American novelist Judith Rossner, and its poignant message struck a resounding chord with me. I think it is a very wise but dreadfully sad observation of the reality of the world I have lived in, and it is relevant to our discussion of this Driver.

Does it matter if we spend our lives failing but do not notice? Assuming we haven't harmed anyone else in the process, is it really important? Although my emotional response still remains one of sadness, my considered answer to this question would be as follows:

'No, free individuals should have as much right to fail as they have to succeed. If they have not noticed their failure, equally they may not have experienced or noticed any accompanying distress.'

Would your answer be different? I can imagine that some religious, political and cultural convictions might shape a different view.

Where we might be in more agreement is in our reaction to a *variation* on this statement which describes another reality with which I am even more familiar:

Many people spend their lives failing and *notice only when they near the end of their lives.*

Assuming that the *awareness* of consistent failure brings

118

severe regret and deep emotional pain, any caring person would consider that fact a just cause for sadness and concern.

Fortunately, when most people reach this enlightened point, there is at least some time left to make amends to themselves, but not even the most brilliant therapist could take away the pain (and often self-abuse) that results from true regret for wasted years.

Our particular concern in this book is that late self-awareness can have either *a devastating effect on motivation* ('What's the point if I've made such a mess of the majority of my life?') or *it can have a life-saving, recharging impact* ('I can't stand this suffering so I *must* change and give myself a chance of at least *some* success').

Of course, there are many 'just in time' solutions available for anyone who has the latter reaction, but they are rarely easy. With hindsight I cannot imagine that anyone would decline regular work on this Driver as a preferred preventative option. People who learn the art of constructive self-criticism need never experience the panic and pressure that inevitably accompany the realization of persistent failure.

So why do so many people leave self-appraisal until the eleventh hour? The answer usually lies in one or more of the following explanations:

- They have *never been taught* this good habit, by example or otherwise.
- Their *experience of criticism* from others was (and often still is) so painful and destructive that all their energy is taken up in coping with that.
- They are simply *so busy* that they think they haven't time.
- Their self-esteem is so low that they *fear* that if they start, they will open up a 'can of worms' which will devour what little motivation they have.
- They are *so busy chastising* themselves for petty 'offenses' or aspects of themselves they cannot change that they never have the time to look at either the big picture or persistent serious patterns.

Whatever the cause, the remedy is much the same. Unlike our last Driver, it is also relatively simple to put into practice, though it does take courage to start. Once the results start making their impact, the task becomes a ritual that few people *want* to give up. This isn't because they have become neurotically addicted to self-flagellation, it is simply because the transitory pain of self-criticism is far outweighed by the more durable pleasures of expanding potential.

 # Tips: Stringent Self-criticism – without Suffocating Self-abuse

❏ Make a short self-criticism session a *daily habit* which is as ritualized as brushing your teeth. (You could even double up on the tasks.) Ask yourself daily these two following questions:
(a) What could I have done better today/yesterday?
(b) What didn't I do which I should have done today/yesterday?

❏ Do not attempt to keep the same standards in every area of your life. A lot of people give themselves unnecessary abuse for not achieving constant perfection. Try *grading your tasks* by 'class' according to their importance to you and the standards you want to achieve (for example, professional skills; marriage and parenting; hobbies; extended family; community; decorating; housework; shopping; gardening; car maintenance). Make sure that the grade you set is a personal one. Reserve the right to change it as *you* deem necessary.

❏ When you are criticized unjustly by others, instead of wasting energy on burying yourself under a mountain of excuses and apologies, simply say something *assertive* like:
'Thank you for reminding me...this is a fault which I am working hard to correct.'
'Yes, I agree I am too...I am keen to stop doing this. Have

you any ideas on how I can do it differently?'
If your response is followed by destructive abuse, use the
technique of *Fogging* to stop the flow (*see Driver 28*).

❑ Don't depress your energy by giving yourself the third
degree over each *minor hiccup*. Instead, calmly note the
persistent ones in your 'black book' and then analyse
them to your heart's content in your regular review
sessions (*see Driver 20*).

❑ Make a habit of *'reframing' self-put-downs* into neutral
positive-action statements rather than kicking yourself for
saying them (for example, 'What an idiot I am, I've just
done it again. Will I ever learn? I'm hopeless...' is more
helpfully expressed as: 'It seems that I've still not learned
how to do...I must note this and look at this next week
and see if I can find a way to...').

Instant Exercise:
Stringent Self-criticism –
without Suffocating Self-abuse

Ask yourself the two questions which I suggested in the first
tip. Note some constructive action you are going to take.

The critic you listen to is yourself.

JACKIE COLLINS

Intolerance of Excuses – without Deafness to their Message

(Notebook page 227)

> *They who excuse themselves, accuse themselves.*
>
> PROVERB

'Ooh, you're hard; I can never get away with it with you.'

When I hear this kind of remark from clients I know that we are on the right track. It means we have reached the stage when I'm in tune with their excuses and (unless they run off in terror of self-exposure!) I know a breakthrough is on the horizon.

This is not a particularly comfortable stage for either party. My clients feel vulnerable without their defences and I have to live with being regarded as 'hard'. But it is undoubtedly easier for me, simply because I can be so confident of a positive outcome.

My confidence in the value of this kind of confrontation has been built from years of experience. I personally refined the art of self-conning years ago. Fortunately, like my courageous clients I too put myself in situations where I knew that I would get honest feedback from people who had the wisdom to 'see through' me and expose my resistant rationalizations. I remember how bitter the pill was to swallow. I never liked listening to what I heard and I argued back with all the might I could muster. My excuses for not taking responsibility for doing what quite obviously needed to be done had become 'truths' which I firmly believed in.

Before taking every positive life-changing step, I have had this kind of major battle with excuses. The moment one argument was defeated and I felt ready to go, another would pop up and block me yet again. Sometimes this process lasted for years! Here are some examples – the general nature of the excuses may ring bells even though the situations may not be ones you have ever experienced:

- I wanted to go to university in my forties to get the degree I had 'been deprived of' in my youth, but it seemed impossible because:
  - – I couldn't afford it
  - – my brain was now 'too slow'
  - – I wouldn't be able to choose a subject
  - – it wouldn't give me any advantages, I'd be better doing...
  - – I'd be too tired to read at night, etc.
- I wanted to write a book on assertiveness but I couldn't because:
  - – as I had never been able to string two sentences together without agonizing angst, I'd get too stressed
  - – others were bound to beat me to it, there was such an obvious need
  - – there were 101 people who were more qualified to write on the subject, etc.
- I wanted to leave my damaging first marriage but I wouldn't because:
  - – it would *ruin* my children's lives
  - – I'd lose credibility as a therapist
  - – I'd never survive the financial burden
  - – I'd lose our joint friends
  - – I'd never find a better husband
  - – I'd become lonely and bitter, etc.

Perhaps I would still be battling with each of these (and many more!) if I hadn't eventually addressed their hidden message. I have now learned that *when we find ourselves being held back by a string of unending excuses, there is usually an underlying problem that needs our attention.* The excuses act as a self-protective mouthpiece for your subconscious, which is truly saying:

- 'You're frightened and you need more support or a good contingency plan.'
- 'Your self-esteem is at a dangerously low ebb and needs a boost.'
- 'You're taking too big a risk, review your agenda and goals.'

Of course, as we have already discussed in other Drivers, sometimes the subconscious gets it wrong. It may be working with out-of-date material. You can test this out by reprogramming it with new, positive, reassuring messages. But if these don't work, do not ever return to kicking yourself.

Tips: Intolerance of Excuses – without Deafness to their Message

❑ Be on *your guard* for excuses when you are either involved in a high-pressure project or under stress for any other reason.

❑ Don't let *bullies* loose on your excuses. Tell them clearly what support or help you need – even if that is to keep their noses out of your psychological business!

❑ Ask supportive but *strong-willed friends* to point out when you start uttering certain classic phrases which may indicate that you *may* have entered the seductive land of rationalization. For example:
'I'll try but…'
'I'm too old/young for that'
'If only…'
'It's so hard…'
'Perhaps one day…'
'When I have more time, I will…'

'When the weather improves, perhaps I'll...'
❑ Pin up the following *quote* – it could help you to keep an eye on your level of commitment.

There's a difference between interest and commitment. When you're interested in doing something, you do it only when it's convenient. When you're committed to something, you accept no excuses, only results.

KENNETH BLANCHARD

❑ Never forget that excuses which do not respond easily to one or two gentle kicks or rational argument, may have a *hidden agenda*.

 ## Instant Exercise:
Intolerance of Excuses – without Deafness to their Message

1 Think of an example from your life (similar to the ones I related earlier) when you too had to battle through excuses before you could achieve one of your goals.
2 List the excuses and mark the ones which are all too familiar. Note what might be the hidden agenda behind each of the most persistent ones.

I'll do today what I could put off doing until tomorrow because I may enjoy doing it and then I can do it again tomorrow!

GAEL LINDENFIELD!

Sincere Self-forgiveness – without Self-inflicted Punishment

(Notebook page 228)

> *Guilt is the most pernicious of human emotions. Also it is the most useless. It does not help the wronged person, and it can only destroy the one who feels it.*
>
> MONICA DICKENS

 I've just calculated that I have probably spent at least a quarter of my life being punished. Even by my own ruthlessly high standards, I know that this degree of suffering was unmerited.

But the judge and jury responsible for this gross miscarriage of justice were none other than a powerful gang assembled from parts of myself!

Let me introduce you to just a few of the ring-leaders:

Goody-gum-drops – the part of me who had her sights firmly set on sainthood and would not overlook even the most minor of my transgressions.

Logic Bore – the part of me who made sure that there was no room for flexibility – three minor sins = three units of minor punishment; one major sin = one major unit of punishment. Happiness and a pure soul could only be achieved with zero scores.

Self-righteous Sinner – the part of me who saw through the rationalizations and would not listen even to a *good* excuse.

Angry Parent – the part of me who always judged me as ungrateful for the help so many wonderful 'rescuers' had graciously given me.

Bossy Bully – the part of me who had perfected the art of defensive intimidation through being a powerless 'put-upon' older sister.

Fearful Child – the part of me whose images of eternal hell and damnation seemed far worse than the temporary 'fires' which I plunged myself into.

Cautious Controller – the part of me who always wanted to make sure that there was plenty of absolving 'grace' in hand in case I was led into temptation yet again.

Although the make-up of my merciless gang was undoubtedly quite unique, I am sure you have met many such 'characters' yourself before. Because my work brings me into contact with so many martyrs, I am constantly meeting similar gang members in other people's cruel psyches. Even after years of personal development work, these fellow self-inflictors, like me, still find it hard to forgive themselves.

But I continue to try because I have learned that self-forgiveness is not a luxury, it is an essential for self-motivators. Here are six good reasons which have helped to convince me. I hope you can add to my list:

Reasons Why Self-forgiveness Is Good for Self-motivators

1 We are often *working on our own* and rarely can we depend on the blessings of others.
2 We are *constantly changing, creating and developing*, and it is impossible to do this without getting it wrong – not just sometimes, but many times.
3 We choose to set *our standards* much higher than an average person would be willing to tolerate.
4 Our *busy schedules* do not allow us much spare time to indulge in wielding the whip.
5 We depend on high levels of *self-esteem*, and this cannot survive for long in purgatory.
6 Our *physical health* needs to be at its very best, and the tension of guilt cripples the immune system.

Tips: Sincere Self-forgiveness – without Self-inflicted Punishment

❑ When you are beating yourself up about something, ask yourself if you would do the same to someone whom you love for the same offence. If the answer is no (and it usually is), ask yourself why you are practising *double standards*?

❑ *Visualize*, in all its specific horrible detail, the most destructive possible outcome of continuing to reprimand yourself for every misdemeanour.

❑ Go to the library and ask to look at the research data on the *effectiveness of punishment*. You'll soon be convinced that it is rarely an efficient way of controlling behaviour. (Rewards and encouragement for effort score consistently much higher.)

❑ When you have let yourself down, the quickest route by far to self-forgiveness is to *make amends*. This path usually points in quite a different direction from the one leading to purgatory.

❑ Remember that a 'naughty thought' is *not* as bad as a 'naughty deed' (whatever anyone else may have told you!). So *never punish yourself for misdemeanours of the mind*, which are unlikely ever to see the light of day.

❑ *Self-punitive statements* are a 'turn-off' for good friends. Ask for helpful feedback before you get too lonely.

Instant Exercise: Sincere Self-forgiveness – without Self-inflicted Punishment

1 Think back to three 'crimes' you have committed, either against yourself or against others.
2 Ask yourself first whether you have had enough living hell over these, and secondly whether or not you still have some work to do in relation to making amends.
3 Finally, write down the action you want to take which will prove to yourself that you are forgiven and can move on.

Driver 26

Personal Power – without Disempowering Others

(*Notebook page 228*)

I don't want to be a passenger in my own life.

DIANE ACKERMAN

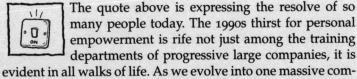 The quote above is expressing the resolve of so many people today. The 1990s thirst for personal empowerment is rife not just among the training departments of progressive large companies, it is evident in all walks of life. As we evolve into one massive competitive world community, it is understandable that we should all be fearing the loss of individual control over our lives. Perhaps it is no coincidence that we are seeing such a rapid expansion of the physical and psychological muscle-building industries!

Like so many of the other Personality Drivers we have already looked at, the relationship between self-motivation and personal power is co-nurturing: Each feeds the other. When we fuel ourselves with inspiration and resolution, we find we actually become more capable of determining the course of our lives. Similarly, if we make a conscious effort to build up empowering traits and skills, our motivation becomes self-firing.

But, although more and more people are openly seeking personal power, they often feel inwardly guilty or worried about doing so. The concept of 'a powerful person' still has negative connotations in our culture. I have known many people hold back their potential simply because they are frightened of becoming 'power-mad'.

I'm not sure if this label 'power-mad' has a definition, but it can certainly conjure up frighteningly real images for most of us. We are instantly reminded of people who will stoop to the very basest acts to assert their strength. We see them doing so not only at the expense of others, but of themselves as well. We also know that an obsessive lust for power can ultimately lead to their own destruction. Some of this century's most powerful Fascist leaders are obvious examples which leap to mind. Most of us also have at least one or two equally vivid images of other bullies lodged in our *personal* memory bank as well.

Personal power can of course also be used in very benign ways as well. Gandhi, Martin Luther King, Mother Theresa and Nelson Mandela are just a few brilliant examples of how the charisma which oozes out of people with this kind of strength can be used positively and motivationally.

But equally, you must also be able to think of numerous examples of this phenomenon in your own life as well. Personal power does not need necessarily to be supported by a position of authority in order to have an effect. I am thinking of the people whose presence is very rarely overlooked because they continually radiate personal energy and strength. You know from the minute they walk into a room that whatever their rank in the official pecking order, they will be a force with which to be reckoned.

Like low-self-esteem, personal powerlessness is so disabling that we need to check that it is not creeping up on us surreptitiously. One of the ways of doing this is to become super-aware of the warning signals that indicate a powerless state.

Warning Signals of Powerless States

Feelings
- ❑ persistent guilt
- ❑ anxiety
- ❑ depression
- ❑ boredom
- ❑ apathy

❏ loneliness
❏ feeling you are misunderstood
❏ feeling ripped off or hard done by
❏ feeling taken for granted
❏ feeling excluded
❏ feeling pressurized

Thoughts

❏ worrying about details and possible negative outcomes
❏ concern for other people's opinion
❏ ruminating about health and death
❏ obsessively mind-reading or trying to understand people
❏ racing or jumbled thoughts
❏ blank mind

Behaviour

❏ doing things that you don't want to do
❏ blaming others incessantly
❏ being over-controlling or over-protective
❏ being over-punitive (of yourself or others)
❏ moaning
❏ asking for help or others' opinion unnecessarily
    or too often
❏ not delegating
❏ being persistently late
❏ spending more than you earn or know to be wise
❏ being 'speechless'

Language

❏ 'He made me...'
❏ 'It would be just my luck'
❏ 'Nobody around here seems to care anymore'
❏ 'You can't seem to trust anyone these days'
❏ 'I suppose I'll just have to put up with it'
❏ 'I know you'll probably be mad at me for saying this'
❏ 'I just had to do it'
❏ 'I don't know what came over me'
❏ 'Isn't it awful the way everybody seems to...?'

- ❏ 'It's not fair, they always...'
- ❏ 'Why me...?'
- ❏ 'If only...'

Non-verbal clues

- ❏ forced smile
- ❏ hurt looks
- ❏ pleading eyes
- ❏ crocodile tears
- ❏ frowns
- ❏ sloppy posture and appearance
- ❏ shuffling feet
- ❏ hand over mouth
- ❏ biting nails
- ❏ picking skin
- ❏ blushing

Health

- ❏ constant backaches or headaches
- ❏ stomach upsets
- ❏ colds
- ❏ sinus problems
- ❏ skin disorders – or any other symptom diagnosed as a stress disorder

If you can put your hand on your heart and declare that you are not likely to experience the above in the next six months, feel free to skip this section and move on to the next Driver.

Tips: Personal Power – without Disempowering Others

❑ When you come face-to-face with people who want to disempower you, remind yourself that however tightly they might tie your hands and deprive you of other kinds of power, no one – but no one – can rob you of this kind of power. Keeping *your dignity in your own eyes* is crucial.

❑ Remember that working on every one of the *other Drivers* in this book is the surest way to ensure that your personal power is kept at its full potential. (It is also the best way of keeping bullies at bay.)

❑ Keep the above *checklist* handy and use from time to time. Show it to supportive friends so they can let you know when they spot signs as well.

❑ The moment you notice that your *feeling* of personal power is slipping, *take responsibility* for doing something about your emotional state, even if you do not consider it was your fault (for example if the nature of your job has changed without your consent; if your children become sick so you are 'forced' to make that a priority and neglect yourself). Use the tips in the other Drivers for firming up your power, such as Driver 3 for positivity, or Driver 5 for your self-esteem.

❑ Make a conscious effort to use *empowering language*, especially when you are talking about a difficult aspect of a task which you cannot avoid. As it may not come naturally to you, script out a few phrases which you can repeat to yourself or others. Even if they sound a bit 'funny', surely that is better than allowing yourself to sink into a powerless state.

For example:

'I'm choosing to do this challenging piece of work to the best of my ability.'

'I refuse to let this get me down. I shall keep at it but make sure that I get a reward at the end.'

'He's difficult to live with but not impossible. I can and

134

will cope even if it means I may need a shoulder to cry on occasionally.'

❏ *Take pride* in possessing personal power and the rewards it brings. Don't give the credit for your successes away, for example to 'luck'. When someone says 'You're so lucky to…', don't reply 'I know' (as most people do!), say: 'It wasn't luck, I *chose* this job/partner/house/team of staff, etc.'

❏ To check that you are not disempowering others, simply ask them for *honest feedback*. But be careful not to accept blame for their own self-disempowering actions (lack of assertiveness, stress, etc.).

 # Instant Exercise: Personal Power – without Disempowering Others

1 Re-read the warning signals above and think of an occasion when your personal power was at a particularly low ebb.
2 Note the actions you took which helped you to regain your feeling of power.

How many cares one loses when one decides not to be something but to be someone.

Coco Gabrielle Chanel

Driver 27

Assertive Directness – without Thoughtless Insensitivity

(Notebook page 229)

Speak fitly, or be silent wisely.

PROVERB

 It's hard to believe that only 15 years ago even the word 'assertiveness' had no meaning for me. Since that time the practice of its art has transformed both my personal and professional life. It has helped me and many thousands of people I have worked with to be themselves and achieve their goals without damaging their self-esteem or storing up mounds of irrational guilt.

But have we had too much of this good thing? The current backlash movement against assertiveness training would propose so. I am now constantly reading articles and listening to conversations which claim that it can divide happy families, disrupt high-achieving schools, spark insurrection in productive offices while also leaving a trail of hurt feelings in its determined wake.

As with the similar attack on therapy which I have already mentioned, when I hear this kind of talk I want to leap to the defence of the 'wonder' techniques which I have spent so many years perfecting. I feel myself aggressively inclined to drown such unfair attacks with an onslaught of counter-evidence. But I try to restrain myself because I know that there are some uncomfortable grains of truth in this criticism, which we must deal with first.

Assertiveness is undoubtedly the kind of behaviour that

I would like to be able to use most of the time. It is much less wasteful of both physical and emotional energy than its alternatives, aggression and passivity. This is why people who have been on assertiveness training courses find themselves more and more attracted to the company of assertive people and much less tolerant of others. This is especially true for people who have found assertiveness late in life and feel they have a lot of catching up to do. They feel life is too short to waste trying to understand or work with or live with people who cannot be as direct and straightforward as they have learned to be.

Previously these new converts to assertiveness have generally spent a disproportionate amount of their lives being *too* considerate of others. I can therefore fully understand why they harden their hearts and sometimes decide to use their new skills to assert their needs in an apparently insensitive manner. To keep ourselves motivated and focused on achieving our own goals, it is easier not to be distracted by the neediness of others.

But, as one of our favourite English clichés reminds us, 'Two wrongs do not make a right.' Assertive techniques and strategies, like any other brilliant empowering tool, *must be used ethically and responsibly*. According to my personal moral code this includes using them only after we have given *due consideration to the feelings and rights of others*.

This does not mean that we can wholly prevent other people from feeling hurt by actions which we deem justified. Every one of us has ultimately to take responsibility for our own emotions. But it does mean that we show our concern and offer help if it is in our power to do so.

Once we have thought through the possible consequences of being direct and open about what we think and feel, *we can also choose not to be assertive*. But, increasingly, I have found that many people feel guilty about using any other behaviour! It is interesting that when I first started teaching assertiveness, I had to spend the first half of any course convincing participants of their right to be assertive. Now I find myself frequently having to do the opposite!

There is certainly 'good' to be gained from using each of these behaviours appropriately. The self-motivated person needs this Driver to help reserve his or her right to take the passive way out sometimes (that is, to do or say nothing). In my first book, *Assert Yourself*, and my recent book *Self-esteem* I have written at more length on this subject, so if the following tips are not sufficient guidance, you could try the programmes in these two books, or join an assertiveness training class.

Tips: Assertive Directness – without Thoughtless Insensitivity

❑ Remember that applying assertiveness is an art and, until you have refined it, you are at risk of using it more bluntly than you would sometimes wish. Practise using your directness in relatively *low-charged emotional situations first*.

❑ Use *'I' statements*
For example:
'Well, it seems that there is not enough...' could become:
'I need...'
'People don't like to be treated...' could become:
'I don't like it when you...'

❑ Use *direct eye contact*, but only about 50 per cent of the time. Most people feel overpowered by any more eye contact than this.

❑ *Encourage others* to be more direct by asking them facilitating questions which take responsibility for your needs, not by making judgemental accusations.
For example:
'Your beating about the bush is driving me mad, can't you get to the point?' could become:
'It would help me to understand better if you could summarize what you want in one or two sentences.'

❑ Make it easy for *people who are less empowered* than you to express their needs by suggesting alternatives, which then give them a choice. Be careful not to patronize or do it for them unnecessarily (even if your time and patience are short!).

For example:

'It must be awful for you not being able to tell her straight. Don't worry, I'll do it for you' could become: 'Are you wanting to ask her...? Or do you want to say...?'

❏ Deal with your unassertiveness *before tension mounts up* and you blurt something out in an aggressive manner, or start to behave manipulatively. (Don't skip the following exercise!)

❏ If you find it difficult to judge how someone might react to your direct approach, try doing a *role play* with a friend, with you taking the other person's part. (This kind of exercise, which I often use in my groups, has helped many people decide to hold back on taking direct confrontative action.)

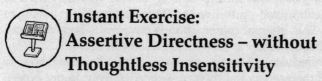

Instant Exercise:
Assertive Directness – without Thoughtless Insensitivity

Think of a request you would like to make to someone, but have not done so yet because you have been afraid of hurting his or her feelings (for example, you'd like to spend Christmas or your holiday in a different way or with different people; you think your good-natured boss or Mum is being over-protective of you, etc.).

Script out a non-threatening way of saying what you need to say, using the tips above and/or other assertiveness strategies you know.

There's a time to speak and a time to be silent.

PROVERB

Driver 28

Skilled Self-protection – without Harmful Aggression

(Notebook page 229)

Skill and confidence are an unconquered army.

PROVERB

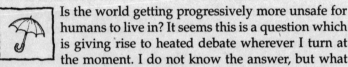 Is the world getting progressively more unsafe for humans to live in? It seems this is a question which is giving rise to heated debate wherever I turn at the moment. I do not know the answer, but what I am sure of is that most people (a) believe that they need to become more self-protective and (b) feel angry about having to do so. This internal combination is dangerous because it can undoubtedly result in harmful aggressive behaviour.

Self-motivators have a special need for knowing how to defend themselves and their projects effectively. In my experience they often meet more than their fair share of destructive criticism and sabotaging abuse simply because they are more successful and self-sufficient and appear content. It happens because we live in a world where just reaching this state is tantamount to waving a red rag to a less fortunate, jealous bull.

Particularly if our path to success has required vast amounts of self-discipline, effort and sometimes deprivation, this kind of reaction will seem very *unfair*. Our natural human response to injustice is to experience a feeling of anger. Unfortunately, this is an emotion which many people still do not know how to manage. For a whole variety of reasons they have never learned how to express this feeling without damaging their relationships with other people and their own self-esteem.

Understandably, they have therefore developed a habit of holding their anger in, which can in the long term be disastrous for their motivation.

For the first half of my adult life I continually repressed my anger in this way. It was a major cause of the apathy, cynicism, depression, self-abusive habits and low immunity which took me several times to the brink of self-destruction. I know that learning how to handle my response to frustration and anger in a more assertive manner was not only a very important key for me to finding the will to live and thrive, but also helped me to protect myself from some of the 'unfair' responses which my later success seemed to spark off in others.

Aggression, in my opinion, should always be seen as a last resort. Although it is sometimes highly justified, it is notoriously wasteful of the resources of time, energy and self-esteem. The successful self-motivator would never, as a general rule, use an aggressive response until assertive approaches have been tried and failed. Such approaches can be learned, but they do require a fair amount of thought and rehearsal before they begin to feel as natural and right as 'lashing out' or 'biting your lip'. In my book *Managing Anger* I suggest many strategies, guidelines and self-help exercises to help develop this Driver. If you haven't read this book, these tips may prove a tempting taster!

 ## Tips: Skilled Self-protection – without Harmful Aggression

❏ Don't waste time and energy arguing with destructive critics, especially if their opinion is of no value or use to you. I have found the technique of *'Fogging'* combined with *Affirmation*, the most effective way to stop them in their tracks.

Fogging combined with affirmation is a technique in which you simply respond calmly with a short sentence which gives the impression that the other person *may* be right, while you inwardly affirm to yourself that he or she is not (for example, say 'You're possibly right, I may be being a bit selfish' while inwardly repeating 'I know that I am a generous enough person').

❑ Get to know your *body signals* which indicate that an angry response has been triggered, so that you can control them early (work on Driver 22 will help).

❑ If you do feel your anger escalating, decide immediately to get some distance from the person or situation until you have *regained emotional control*. Never try to resolve conflict while your blood is boiling.

❑ When you are in a position of having to work or live with people who continually take advantage of your good-will, resources, time or space, *take responsibility for releasing your physical tension safely* before confronting them with a well-prepared and rehearsed assertive response. Only ever sweep your frustration and anger under the carpet in emergency situations, and *always* retrieve and deal with them as soon as you can. (Make a note of these feelings if you are in the habit of conveniently forgetting about them after the moment has passed!)

❑ Before going into any situation where you are likely to need to protect yourself, *talk through your strategy* with a supportive friend. You could even role-play to practise responding to the worst possible attack.

❑ Never underestimate the power of a *verbal attack* to demotivate you. It is often easier to protect yourself from a physical attack, because it is much more socially acceptable to be seen to do so. Remember your subconscious receives the message even if you think you are 'above' listening to it!

Instant Exercise: Skilled Self-protection – without Harmful Aggression

Examine the current state of your Achilles' heel for a moment. (Don't forget that it is a living part of you and changes as you grow and with your circumstances.)

Ask yourself these questions:

1 What are some of my present 'touchy' areas?
2 How could I protect myself if these were to come under attack? (Use assertive words and action.)

Perpetually Learning – without Devaluing Own Wisdom

(Notebook page 230)

> *Nothing in the world is more dangerous than sincere ignorance and conscientious stupidity.*
>
> MARTIN LUTHER KING

 There are only a few things in life which can give me as great a buzz as learning. It has the power to lift me out of the deepest doldrums, and I find the thought of being deprived of its stimulation quite frightening. Recently I read about some research that has proved that when we learn something new, we actually generate extra brain cells. You can imagine how pleased I was to find such a perfect justification for further indulgences in my craving for learning!

But however pleasurable the process of learning is for me, I know that in order to be totally satisfying 'the high' that it generates in me must be followed by some purposeful or creative action. Having talked to many other successful self-motivators on this subject, I am convinced that it is this additional aspect of the addiction that makes it such a useful tool for generating motivation.

I am aware that for many people learning has not the same addictive appeal. You may have lost your natural curiosity and thirst for knowledge and skills. Perhaps it was destroyed or contaminated as far back as childhood, through unhappy or unsatisfying educational experiences at school or at home. I have found this to be especially true among people who are naturally drawn towards self-managed careers. They frequently recall having been independent and practical or creative children who did not thrive in the rigid academic environments in which they were educated. Understandably this left them with either irrational anxieties about their own learning ability or more general feelings of suspicion concerning education and training.

But in building up this Driver there isn't any danger that you will be seduced into eternal studentship. I am not suggesting that you need to be involved in any kind of purist scholarship simply for its own sake. This Driver is about *developing ongoing educational habits which will expand your brain cells and enhance your potential to achieve your down-to-earth goals*. But, looking at the bigger picture, you will not be the only beneficiary. The world undoubtedly gains from people who take pride in their own growing wisdom and are continually looking for ways to use it constructively.

 # Tips: Perpetually Learning – without Devaluing Own Wisdom

❑ If you have lost your thirst for learning, start by doing something which is of *interest to you and builds on your existing strengths*. Don't worry too much about what use you will put it to at this stage. Once our brain cells start growing, it's amazing how many new ideas we get for ways to apply our knowledge!

❑ If you found traditional education boring or too stressful, don't start with a formal course, even if you think that is what you need. Renew your enthusiasm for education by trying for a while one of the many *innovative, fun* ways to learn that are now available (cassettes, CD-ROMs, videos, activity holidays, living museums, dramatherapy training – not to mention self-help books like this!).

❑ Keep experimenting until you find the course or style of teaching that *suits you*. (The only educational experiences

I have ever regretted were ones where I 'stuck with' boring or poorly taught courses or dry, stuffy books.)

❑ Always take time to find a way of relating any theory and facts you learn to your *own personal experience of life*. Don't be tempted to cram them in just to acquire a certificate or exam. That kind of learning is great for robots, but it quickly deadens the human spirit and brain.

❑ Don't ever be *ashamed* of your level of knowledge and try to 'get by', afraid of asking questions. Instead, repeat frequently to yourself the following assertive right:
'I have a right not to know or understand.'
– and then do whatever you need to acquire the knowledge. Often this means just summoning up the courage to be seen appearing stupid or a swot! The buzz you'll get from learning soon obliterates the pain of being judged by ignorant others.

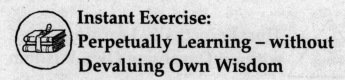

Instant Exercise:
Perpetually Learning – without Devaluing Own Wisdom

Complete this sentence six times:
'I would love to know more about…'
Choose one of your six to base a resolution on.
An example might be:
'I would love to know more about Thai cookery.'
Your resolutions could then include:

'I will go to a Thai restaurant/get a book on the subject/ invite some friends round to sample my experiments with Thai dishes.'

Seriously Focused – without Humourless Solemnity

(Notebook page 230)
I doubt if many of you reading this book will need to work on the serious side of this Driver. If you have taken the trouble to read this far it is unlikely that your earnestness is in question. But how lively is the fun side of you?

So many people find it difficult to let go and enjoy themselves that many therapists like myself have started to introduce courses on the theme of having fun. In Britain, a stress specialist colleague of mine, Robert Holden, has even set up a Laughter Clinic funded by the National Health Service and has written self-help books on the subject.

But humour and fun need not be just pleasant ways of destressing ourselves after the grind of work is done. When they are integrated into our daily working schedule they can radically improve productivity. When preparing for a recent training session on motivation with senior executives, I identified some reasons why fun should be taken more seriously by management. These reasons also hold true for anyone or any group who is keen to maximize their chances of achieving their goals, however frivolous or serious.

Laughter and Fun

– are good for self-motivation because they:

- **Stimulate positive thinking**
  - – We know that laughter stimulates endorphins, which in turn give us positive feelings even when we are surrounded by negativity.
- **Release tension**
  - – We have fewer aches and pains and can therefore be sure we will be able to concentrate more efficiently.
- **Increase energy levels**
  - – A 'good laugh' stimulates the production of adrenalin and endows us with renewed physical strength and mental energy.
- **Improve general health**
  - – Research has shown that regular 'shots' of fun and laughter boost our body's own immune system and help us to heal more quickly.
- **Stimulate creative thinking**
  - – Humour starts the right brain working, which as we know is the centre of our creativity, intuition and inspiration.
- **Widen perspective**
  - – After seeing the 'funny side' of things we often alter our viewpoint. So humour can be a good challenge to a perspective that has sunk into a rut.
- **Strengthen relationships**
  - – Sharing fun times together is undoubtedly one of the quickest ways of breaking the ice and establishing closer, more committed professional and personal partnerships.
- **Offer incentive**
  - – Who wouldn't be more inclined to 'get on with it' if the 'it' could guarantee fun as well as success?

Tips: Seriously Focused –
without Humourless Solemnity

❏ Keep a book of *humorous quotations* and cartoons at your desk, bedside or on your coffee table and dip into it regularly.

❏ When you're feeling jaded or beset with worry, imagine what *your favourite comedy star* would say if he or she could whisper in your ear.

❏ Stimulate your ability to see the funny side of serious subjects by regularly watching *comedy programmes* which do just this (political satire, sitcoms about people usually stereotyped in the media, such as vicars, single parents or the elderly).

❏ When faced with an 'unsolvable' problem, take ten minutes to *imagine that you are a comedy writer* commissioned to use this situation as material. What style would suit it (slapstick/farce/cartoon/clown mime/musical/sitcom/silent movie, etc.)? Whom might you cast in the central roles? What might its grand climax be?

❏ Spend some time with young children, or watch a few of the TV shows aimed at them.

❏ Make it a rule that at least one *lunch break* a week should be spent in a fun way.

❏ Before starting to collaborate with others on a project, make sure that you *schedule some time for light relief* together. (Even if your senses of humour are very different, try to find something to do together which does not feel deadly serious.)

❏ When you have a particularly important project on the go, set aside extra time to spend with *people who have the courage to tease you benignly*, even when your mood is foul. (My own home is full of them!)

❏ Buy yourself a *cassette* for the car or your personal stereo of recorded laughter – it certainly is infectious and is a brilliant tool for a quick-fix.

Instant Exercise: Seriously Focused – without Humourless Solemnity

Think back over the last month and count how many times you have had:

- a deep laugh
- at least two uninterrupted hours of fun
- lunch or a drink after work with people who can stimulate the fun side of you

Driver 31

Sensibly Self-nurturing – without Spurning Support

(Notebook page 231)
Looking after the welfare of Number 1 is so plainly essential for sustaining self-motivation that any discussion I might get into on the subject would mean stating the obvious. Instead, I thought I would make my point by asking you to fill in the following short questionnaire.

Self-nurture Checklist

Answer *honestly* yes or no to the following statements:

- ☐ I have adequate sleep to meet the demands of my body.
- ☐ My diet is as nutritional as I need it to be.
- ☐ When buying a chair for myself I would give more consideration to comfort and support than style.
- ☐ When buying a car I would choose the safest one I could afford.
- ☐ When choosing a holiday I give top priority to how well it will recharge me.
- ☐ The environments in which I work and live are as unstressful as I could possibly make them.
- ☐ I say 'no' to requests which I know will over-stretch my physical, mental or emotional energy.
- ☐ I delegate easily whenever it is appropriate without needing to check the other person's progress.

❏ I seek good advice readily and never hold back for fear of being a burden or seeming inadequate.
❏ I ask for emotional support from others even when I currently have nothing to give in return.

If you had eight honest 'yes' answers, I am full of admiration. If you had ten out of ten, I am not sure that I would believe you!

Perfect self-care is an ideal that no one I have yet met seems able to reach. I know that I need constant reminders to keep mine healthy, even though I would guess that (because it's my business!) my commitment in this area is well above average.

Tips: Sensibly Self-nurturing – without Spurning Support

❏ Accept that *high-pressure activity should always be matched with better than average self-nurturing and support.*
❏ Make sure that there is *room for flexibility* in your self-care programme, and that it is not bound to strict routine.
❏ Make a habit of *balancing states of over-tiredness with extra rest*, as quickly as you possibly can.
❏ Before entering a supermarket, set a specific numbered *limit on the non-nutritional indulgences* you will allow yourself.
❏ When allowing yourself periods of slapdash, lazy eating, always make sure you take *vitamin supplements.*
❏ Make *routine hygiene* an opportunity for pleasant self-caring (for example, is a bath more self-nurturing for you than a shower? Is your bathroom devoted to luxurious bathing? Are the scents of your soaps, after-shave and eau de toilette pleasurable to *your* senses?)
❏ After a *setback*, routinely give yourself a dose of extra self-nurturing before moving on to the next project.
❏ Err on the side of *over-delegation* and encourage others to take responsibility for deciding whether tasks can be accomplished or not.

❑ Be clear about the *specific kind of support* you can get from each of your friends and colleagues. Don't depend on a best friend to be 'Jack of all trades' in this respect. Know whom you can call on to be calm in a crisis; give practical help; mop up tears; laugh it off with you; fight on your behalf, etc.

❑ Steer clear of advice-givers when you are seeking *emotional* support. It is *good listeners* who will be of most help.

Instant Exercise: Sensibly Self-nurturing – without Spurning Support

1 Imagine you were given a large cash sum to be spent on a weekend of pure self-nurturing just for you. What would you do with it?

2 Summarize the essential elements which would make this weekend a caring experience for you.

Driver 32

Seeker of Solitude – without Reclusive Aloofness

(Notebook page 231)

> *Everyone needs some human relationships but everyone also needs some kind of fulfilment which is relevant to themselves alone.*
>
> ANTHONY STORR

 Belonging to a group is undoubtedly a strong motivational force. This is why so many successful organizations are happy to spend vast resources building up team spirit and a sense of group identity. But with the exception of the very highest achievers, few people appreciate how important for *sustained* motivation it is to balance group activities with equally energizing periods of solitude.

Solitude, it now seems, is harder both to find and to take. But I know that I cannot afford to allow myself to be daunted by this challenge.

Not only do I now thoroughly enjoy my time on my own, if I lost it I know that I would achieve much less. The following are some of the main reasons why solitude has become so important to me:

- It helps me to be more *self-aware*. Often it isn't until I am alone that my true feelings begin to emerge. Getting in touch with my true feelings in this way helps me to reassess my *priorities*.

- Without the distraction of outside stimuli, my own thoughts develop more freely and I return to problems with a much *clearer sense of direction*.
- Peace and tranquility stimulate my imagination and inspire my *creativity*.
- Solitude *physically recharges* me, so I am able to withstand much greater degrees of pressure.
- It builds my sense of *personal security* by reinforcing my belief that I could survive any amount of loss or separation.
- It boosts my *self-esteem* to know that I have been able to have a great time in my own company.
- It gives me time to reflect on, and cater for, *my own needs* without being distracted by those of others, which I regularly perceive to be greater.
- It gives me the opportunity to indulge in my sometimes 'quirky' ways of *rewarding* myself, without the pressure of having to cope with being considered odd or selfish. (No, I am not going to reveal what they are!)

For many years I couldn't make use of the benefits solitude offers me because, although I knew I was irresistibly attracted towards it, I assumed that I was either sick or selfish to want it. I regularly lied and made excuses to get it. ('I have to wash my hair tonight'/'I have a lot of work to catch up on'/'The children don't want to go,' etc.!) Having achieved it, I then began to feel either guilty or desperately lonely!

I don't know how many other people in the world share this particular neurosis, but I do know that Anthony Storr's brilliant book *Solitude* is one of the most borrowed from my own library.

It is likely that the introverts among you may be more keen to work on this Driver. Perhaps because our society is much more hospitable and encouraging to extroverts, I find that often they have not even noticed what they are missing by staying too firmly in the 'group-belonging' camp.

Getting the right balance is hard for all of us, but it certainly does seem to be one of the skills that successful self-motivators are likely to have mastered. They manage to have very satisfying relationships, ranging from passionate partners through to interesting acquaintances, while still maintaining and enjoying their periods of solitude.

> *The fear of loneliness has been like a ball and chain restraining ambition…as much of an obstacle to a full life as persecution, discrimination or poverty.*
>
> THEODORE ZELDIN

 # Tips: Seeker of Solitude – without Reclusive Aloofness

❏ Don't look over your shoulder for guidance on the right balance for you; take some solitude and use it to reflect on your state of happiness and degree of success. Adapt your life to meet *your current needs*.

❏ Before going to sleep each night, or as soon as you wake up, repeat the following *assertive rights* until they are firmly lodged in your subconscious. Only stop when you have started to act as though you believe them.
'I have a right to be alone and independent'
'I have a right to privacy'

❏ If you are not used to intervals of solitude, start with very *short periods*. I often suggest just ten minutes a day for the first two weeks.

❏ When you first start giving yourself time alone, *expect to feel some negative feelings*. These usually come from the child part of you that is frightened. Do not chastise yourself for being 'silly' (that will make the feelings worse), instead play the 'counsellor' to your inner child. Try asking yourself questions to find out what the fear is about. Is it an out-of-date fear (perhaps dating back from times in your childhood when loneliness was enforced upon you) or is it more current (perhaps you have neglected your friends and family recently, or they are beginning to reject you)? When you have discovered the reason, do something positive to reassure yourself and allay the fear (such as affirmations or an action plan).

❑ Expect some people to question your requests for periods of seclusion, and be ready with your assertive replies. But don't forget that, assuming you are not neglecting your duties and responsibilities, *you do not need to justify your right to solitude* to anyone.

❑ If you find it difficult to say 'no' to invitations, use assertiveness and the *Broken Record* technique to ensure that you don't get drawn into an argument or discussion in the first place.

This technique involves repeating calmly over and over again one phrase giving a clear message until it has sunk in! Believe me, it does work and it is far better than lying or exhausting yourself with circular arguments. For example: 'Thank you for the offer, but *no, I am staying at home this weekend*...I appreciate you're disappointed but *I am staying at home this weekend*...I don't want to discuss my reasons, I have decided that *I am staying at home this weekend.*'

❑ Keep a special file or section in your diary or *Notebook* for use in your times alone – you'll be surprised at how quickly it can get filled with ideas.

❑ If your partner sees your request for time on your own as a sign that the relationship is deteriorating, put him or her right! All the research indicates that the closest and most lasting partnerships are those where each partner is able to maintain a good degree of independence. *Too much togetherness* is bad news for long-term relationships.

❑ Try an alternative holiday at a *retreat* centre. Many more are available now, even ones which are not necessarily religiously orientated. (Look in the Activity Holidays section of the paper or in personal development magazines for addresses.)

❑ By using meditation and assertiveness it is possible to achieve a high degree of solitude *while still in the company of others*. My favourite way of achieving this is to choose to travel by train whenever I can and politely refusing to engage with any of the other passengers in conversation.

Instant Exercise:
Seeker of Solitude –
without Reclusive Aloofness

1 Draw a pie chart to represent the balance in your life between solitude and time spent with others.
2 Using a dotted line or coloured pen, draw the lines where you would prefer them to be.
3 Note down what action you can take to give yourself some extra solitude.

Nothing can be accomplished without solitude.

PABLO PICASSO

Revelling in Success – without Fear of Failure

(Notebook page 232)

> *The common idea that success spoils people by making them vain, egotistical and self-complacent is erroneous. On the contrary, it makes them for the most part humble, tolerant and kind.*
>
> SOMERSET MAUGHAM

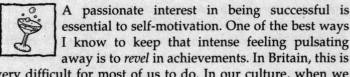 A passionate interest in being successful is essential to self-motivation. One of the best ways I know to keep that intense feeling pulsating away is to *revel* in achievements. In Britain, this is very difficult for most of us to do. In our culture, when we have reached our heights the traditional expectation is that (if we want to remain 'nice' and not let success 'spoil' us) we should:

– act as though we have not changed (even though we feel ten times our previous size and are now brimming with new confidence and positive bonhomie!)
– make only very modest adjustments to our lifestyle (even though our pot of gold may be spilling over into the bank's own vaults!)
– maintain our loyalty to old friends (even though they continually make sly jealous digs at us)
– humbly give the major credit for our achievement away to others (even though inwardly we know they did nothing, or even tried to sabotage our success)

– be satisfied with what we have already achieved, especially if it is much more than others (even though we are now inspired to scale even dizzier heights)

– keep our celebrations discreetly low-key (even though the rest of the town would also welcome a chance to paint the place red)

But there is another factor that also inhibits many people from shouting from the roof-tops about their achievements, and that is a kind of superstition which has been built up around that well-known saying,

'Pride comes before a fall.'

With this saying lurking around in their subconscious (if not on the lips of their loved ones!), self-congratulation feels risky. There is an underlying fear that fate will inevitably punish a show of pride with subsequent resounding failure. An affectation of humble self-effacement is, understandably, a preferable option to such a harsh reprimand from destiny.

But avoidance of the pain of failure *can* be a great motivating force. For some people it has even more 'pulling power' than the lure of the pleasures of success. John Paul Getty is a notable example:

> *Hatred of failure has always been part of my nature and, I suppose, one of the most motivating forces in my life. It's not that I love success for its own sake.*

But, trying to avoid failure because we detest it is very different from avoiding it because we *fear* it. Successful self-motivators will not allow themselves to be frightened. Instead of worrying over any negatives that fate may have in store they develop a 'fighting' strategy which they use to transform their failure into another success.

> *Failure is, in a sense, the highway to success, in as much as every discovery of what is false leads us to seek earnestly after what is true.*
>
> JOHN KEATS

Double your rate of failure...Failure is a teacher – a harsh one, perhaps, but the best...you can be discouraged by failure or learn from it.

THOMAS WATSON – FOUNDER OF IBM

I reserve the right to fail as fundamental; it allows clear-headed people with resilient souls to rebound and go further than they ordinarily would.

BERNARD TAPIE – SUCCESSFUL FRENCH INDUSTRIALIST

I cannot guarantee that with this Driver you will be able to write another *Ode on a Grecian Urn* or chair a multi-national company, but I am confident that your motivation will be enhanced. When failure holds no fear for us, we can bask in the inspirational glory of success to our heart's content!

 Tips: Revelling in Success – without Fear of Failure

❑ For six months or so, drop the word 'failure' from your vocabulary. Use alternatives such as 'temporary setback', 'challenge', 'I've just been through a learning curve!' (If they sound a bit odd – so what?! You're going to benefit in the long run.)

❑ Use affirmations and positive self-talk to counteract worry about failure. (For example: 'I am capable of success' / 'I enjoy learning from any experience' / 'The journey can be just as rewarding as the outcome.')

❑ Use your imagination to visualize yourself being successful or, when failure looks inevitable, coping with it in a dignified, competent manner.

❑ Celebrate and reward every minor success *en route* to your goal in an appropriate manner (*see Driver 36*).

❑ Make detailed plans for celebrating your success as soon as you start working towards your goal. Show them to supportive friends and ask them to enter dates in their diary. If such plans have already been made you will be less tempted to listen to the negative messages which I mentioned earlier, which seem to flood our subconscious mind as soon as success knocks at the door.

❑ Make a big fuss of other people's success, and encourage them after failure. (But don't forget to give them some healing time to work through their grief.)

❑ For every project or risk you undertake make sure that you have a contingency plan. Here is a formula you could photocopy and use:

Personal Contingency Plan

Possible problem: ....
What is likely to be my immediate emotional reaction?
....
....

What are likely to be my dominant feelings once the initial shock has subsided?
....
....

What action can I take to ensure that I keep in good emotional health during this period?
....
....

What action will I need to take to ensure that I maintain my physical health during this period?
....
....

What particular personal strengths can I use to cope positively with such a problem?
....
....

Which of my skills are most likely to be of use to me at such a time?

....

....

Which of my self-sabotaging habits will I need to be on my guard against?

....

....

What positive action can I take to ensure that my behaviour is consistently self-supportive and under my control?

....

....

To whom can I turn to for the very best support?
1. emotional (comfort)

....

....

2. practical (resources)

....

....

3. intellectual (ideas)

....

....

Is there anyone whose company or advice I should be wary of at such a time?

....

....

What do I need to do to acquire any new skill or gain any new information which will enable me to cope more effectively?

....

....

What positive benefits can I (and/or others) gain as a result of such an experience?

....

....

Instant Exercise:
Revelling in Success –
without Fear of Failure

1 Try to think of a success you have had in the past which
   deserved more celebration than it actually got. You must
   be able to find at least one, even if you have to dig deep
   into your memory bank. For example, you could choose:
   – a success at school which no one appreciated, perhaps
   because they didn't know hard you had to try
   – one which happened in a long series of tiny steps
   which seemed too insignificant to make much of, such
   as parenting a child
   – one which was overlooked simply because there wasn't
   enough time to revel.
2 Plan the party! (For the purposes of strengthening this
   Driver it should involve *at least* one other person.)

*Defeat may be a stepping stone or stumbling block according to
the way you accept it.*

NAPOLEON HILL

Driver 34

Scrupulously Self-healing – without Dismissing Comfort

(Notebook page 232)

Successful self-motivators are undoubtedly strong, resilient people. You can depend on them to bounce back after any number of hurts, setbacks, mistakes and failures. Others often look at them enviously and say or think:

'I wish I could be as tough and didn't get so hurt and upset...if that had happened to me, I'd have been devastated. I could never have carried on the way he/she did.'

Self-motivators are 'hardened' survivors not because they are inhuman robots without feeling. As I discussed in Driver 22, they are usually people who put a high value on their emotions but do not want their feelings to be in the driving seat of their lives. They bounce back because they are motivated to bounce back. They are able to do this not because they deny or repress their feelings but because they *know how to heal effectively* from their hurts and losses and *take very active steps* to make sure that they do so.

In my years of work as a psychotherapist I have of course met very many hundreds of emotionally wounded people. But I am sure you would be surprised to know how many emotionally hurt people I meet nowadays in my work with highly successful people. When I am leading courses for companies and professional organizations on subjects like self-confidence and assertiveness, managing pressure and change or effective communication and leadership, I find that I am regularly asked to take a diversion from the scheduled programme so that we can cover the subject of emotional healing.

Here are some typical examples of the demotivating blocks to success at work caused by unhealed wounds. I am sure you will recognize many and can perhaps still empathize with these types of emotional pain:

- *uncharacteristic pessimism* caused by unhealed disappointments (as from lost business or a past redundancy)
- *fear of using assertive skills* caused by unhealed resentment from having your personal power stamped upon by a parent or teacher
- *inability to work effectively with certain people* because their behaviour is innocently opening up a wound of unexpressed resentment from a past relationship
- *lowered productivity* because so much energy is being used to suppress the pain of past bereavement or separation

These kinds of wounds can, of course, also block our motivation in our personal lives. For example, we may:

- *not be able to persist with dieting* because of the enduring pain of having our self-image knocked by someone in the past
- *procrastinate over finding new friends* because we are unable to shake off the grief of losing someone special
- *be unable to thrive in our chosen sport* because we are blocked by unexpressed bitterness about not being selected for the school team

Why do some people seem to heal much better than others from emotional wounds?

The short general answer to this question is that some people:

A may not have been taught how to heal during their social learning years in childhood (through practice and example)
B may never have appreciated its value and realized that it is a skill and art which can be learned as an adult.

I have identified five essential stages that we need to work through if we are to complete the healing process well enough to ensure that we will not become emotionally blocked. There also appear to be two other optional stages which will then help us to become 'super healed'.

Strategy for Emotional Healing

Essential Stages

1 **Exploration**
   – finding out more about the exact nature of our hurt or loss, usually achieved through self-reflection or discussion
2 **Expression**
   – letting our feelings surface, sensing them physically and allowing them at least some minimal release
3 **Comfort**
   – allowing ourselves to be soothed either verbally or non-verbally by someone else who genuinely accepts, and possibly empathizes with, our emotional state
4 **Compensation**
   – giving ourselves at least some recompense for the hurt even if we cannot fully repair the 'damage' or give ourselves full restitution
5 **Perspective**
   – standing back and looking at the experience objectively and possibly finding out what (knowledge, understanding, potentially positive outcomes) we could gain from it

Bonus Stages

6 **Channelling**
   – finding a constructive outlet for using the experience to help either ourselves or others
7 **Forgiveness**
   – wiping the slate squeaky clean by shaking hands either literally or metaphorically with the person(s) or thing(s) responsible for wounding us.

Tips: Scrupulously Self-healing – without Dismissing Comfort

❏ *Each time you experience a wound* to your emotions (however small), check that you take yourself through at least the first five stages outlined above.

❏ *Don't be tempted to skip any stages* even if one feels uncomfortable or 'unnecessary'.

❏ Reflect on whether you are one of the *types likely to make the mistake* of rushing headlong into certain stages. For example:

Perspective – seductive to the *intellectuals* who feel that once they understand why or how, the problem is over
Channelling – seductive to the *workaholics* who believe that hard distracting work or activity is an emotional 'cure-all'
Forgiveness – seductive to the would-be saints among us

Take particular care if you would place yourself in any of these categories.

❏ *Talk* about these various stages to people who may be interested in helping you learn to heal more effectively. Remember that we often do not notice our own worst emotional habits.

Instant Exercise:
Scrupulously Self-healing –
without Dismissing Comfort

1 Write out and memorize the following sentence. The first
  letter of each word is the same as each of the emotional
  healing stages.

Every Emotional Cut
Can Produce Creative Fruit

2 Using these five stages, review *two* emotional wounds –
  one small and one large. Assess where you are in terms
  of being healed and what you may need to do in order
  to complete the process effectively.

Driver 35

Amply Self-rewarding – without Rejecting Recognition

(Notebook page 233)
Rewards should be part of your staple *daily* diet of psychological nutrients. I believe that they are *the* most essential food for sustaining long-term motivation. How many have you *given to yourself* during the past week?

Why do we tend to starve ourselves of this crucial source of emotional nourishment? The following reasons are the most common which I have come across. As you read them, note the ones with which you identify. Every one holds some meaning for me, so it's no wonder that I have had to work so hard on building up this Driver.

- *Ignorance:* not realizing just how vital positive reinforcement (jargon for 'reward'!) is to the process of learning and motivation
- *Fear of becoming 'spoiled':* thinking that 'good character' can be destroyed by too many rewards (possibly as a result of hearing too many variations on 'you'll get too big for your boots' or 'you'll get complacent'!)
- *Guilt:* being very aware of the deprivation and lack of success of others and mistakenly believing that holding back on rewards has the power to make the less fortunate feel better
- *Negativity:* inability to feel positive about success because you are thinking 'It probably won't last/pride comes before a fall,' etc.
- *Misunderstanding:* believing that the only worthwhile rewards should be given by others, or that they should only be

awarded on the completion of major successes and final goals

- *Lack of options:* shortage of ideas for meaningful and satisfying rewards, partly because the subject is not allocated enough thoughtful attention. A typical comment would be: 'I should have given myself a reward, I did deserve it. I suppose I just couldn't think of anything to do for myself at the time and then I got caught up in the next thing'
- *Pressure of time:* managing a life full of such tight schedules that reward time always stays at the bottom of the 'to do' list
- *Fear of others' bad opinion:* thinking that everyone in the world will disapprove of self-rewarding behaviour when in fact the reality is that the majority are green with envy

Nowadays no one should be dependent on others for rewards. We are currently witnessing a depletion of the traditional 'carrots' such as pay-rises, promotions, honours and medals. There even seems to be a shortage of simple 'thank-yous' as everyone becomes more competitive, anxious and busy. If we are lucky enough to get recognition from others, no matter how late in the day it may arrive, we should accept this willingly as well. However, our first task must always be to *reward ourselves*.

 ## Tips: Amply Self-rewarding – without Rejecting Recognition

❑ Once you have identified your own 'reasons' for not giving yourself enough rewards, *compose appropriate affirmations* to use as supportive self-talk. For example:
Misunderstanding: 'I believe that it is important to reward small achievements. I can encourage others by my rewarding behaviour.'
Pressure of time: 'Rewards are one of my priorities. I always make time for my rewards.'

❑ Start rewarding yourself for *small achievements* each day until the habit is well and truly entrenched and you can cope with the 'bigger stuff'!

❑ Don't forget that self-rewards for *effort* are perhaps even more important than those given for success, because often the latter brings its own intrinsic pleasure or recognition from others.

❑ Use *creative visualization* to overcome any embarrassment you feel over accepting praise or recognition from others. Take yourself into a physically relaxed state and then use your imagination to conjure up pictures of yourself calmly taking deserved praise and reward from others.

❑ If you find you are not getting enough deserved recognition, use your *assertive skills* to ask directly for it. Don't be tempted to use sarcasm or other aggressive methods, which never lead to believable, high-quality recognition.

❑ If your *due recognition is denied* in spite of your assertive request, immediately *give yourself a reward* for effort and then objectively assess whether you need or want to take further action (about whether or not this is the right relationship/job, etc. for you to be in).

❑ Never make important decisions in the immediate wake of being denied your due recognition or reward. Take yourself through the *Emotional Healing* process first (*see Driver 34*).

❑ Use *holidays* as a way of rewarding yourself. Nowadays too many people feel they have to use holidays for other purposes (catching up on boring admin work/lightening their load of parental guilt/spring cleaning, etc.). A member of one of my groups was having difficulty last summer in giving herself a rewarding holiday. We helped her give herself her deserved break by collectively making a 'goals for holidays' list, similar to the one in the following exercise. I am pleased to say that by the time the next holiday period arrived she had become a reformed character and unashamedly booked herself into a peaceful retreat!

Instant Exercise:
Amply Self-rewarding –
without Rejecting Recognition

1 Read the following list while reflecting on your last break (either a weekend or longer spell).

Goals for Holidays

- To give myself:
  - treats
  - relaxation
  - extra sleep
  - a mental recharge
  - nutritional boost
  - stimulation of change
  - an opportunity to be myself (not play roles)
  - time to 'remodel' myself (new clothes, hairstyle, fitter body, etc.)
  - relaxed time schedules
  - time to please myself
  - opportunities for daydreaming and fantasizing
  - fun
  - creative stimulation
  - freedom from emotional restraint
  - chance to be looked after
  - choice to be with people I like
  - experiences which bring me back down to earth
  - time to reflect and reassess goals

2 Tick three goals to which you intend giving priority during your next break.
3 Copy the list; add to it and put it in your holiday file or suitcase. You can take it with you as a reminder!

Self-motivation

The greatest reward in terms of psychological satisfaction comes through recognition – being seen to have achieved and having that achievement publicly recognized.

ALLEN CARMICHAEL

Driver 36

Inwardly Driven – without Scorning Incentives

(Notebook page 233)
You've reached the last lap! I hope you're not mentally exhausted at the thought of all the personal development work you may have set yourself to do.

It is undoubtedly a challenging task to build and sustain good quality self-motivation. There is no escaping the fact that the task is primarily our own responsibility, but there are still a few enticing external incentives around! As with rewards from others, these should not be piously disregarded once we have reached the lofty heights of total self-reliance. Even if we do not *need* offers of extra money, promotions, silver cups or even just gratitude, we should not kick such 'gift-horses' away.

Perhaps you cannot yet imagine yourself doing anything quite so daft as to turn down incentives from others, but I have seen it happen many times. Indeed, when I first experienced genuine psychological and economic independence I began to do so myself. I can still hear myself rejecting incentives with responses like these:

'Thanks for the offer but it's not necessary. I'm doing this for me.'

'No thanks, you don't need to give anything to me to reciprocate in any way, the work gives me enough satisfaction in itself.'

It's a great relief to have control over this neurotic quirk. I can now lap up the stimulation of inducements without fear that they will reduce my own internal drive. I hope that when you have reached the stage when you know your self-motivation is sturdy and durable you will also enjoy the fun of competing for the carrots as well. When you feel ready to start building up this Driver, here are a few tips.

Tips: Inwardly Driven – without Scorning Incentives

❏ Keep checking that the incentives you are using are in line with your *current needs*. Your bank balance might have fortunately outgrown the need for a little extra money and you might now be more motivated by an opportunity to learn a new skill. (Remember Driver 2.)

❏ Keep *reminders* of your incentives in constant view (such as a picture of what you would buy with the extra money or a drawing of the diploma you will receive at the end of the course).

❏ There is never any harm in *asking people to give you a greater incentive*. You can explain that you will do a very good job without it, but that you might do a brilliant job with better pay/extra holidays/a promotion or a grander prize. It's not bribery, it's just probably the truth!

❏ When you start *blaming* your apathy on the incentive for its inadequacy or its donor for his or her lack of generosity, it may be time to *start giving some of your self-motivation Drivers a boost*. (But don't let a fear of greediness stop you from asking for a better incentive as well!)

Instant Exercise: Inwardly Driven – without Scorning Incentives

1 Note down a few of the most effective incentives you have experienced in the whole of your life.
2 Ask yourself these questions:
   – Do I have similar incentives in my life now?
   – If not, why not?
   – If they might help, could I give any aspect of these to myself in the near future or would I prefer to concentrate on building up my inner Drivers first?

Never look a gift horse in the mouth.

PROVERB

2

Quick-fix Strategies

How to Recharge Your
Self-motivation after a Setback

Even the most consistently highly self-motivated people do have some setbacks. As they are the first to admit, usually these are of their own making – but just occasionally they may have been played a quirky negative hand by fate. But an important difference between them and many other less successful people is that *they do not allow themselves to get submerged by guilt, remorse or despair at injustice.* Instead they set about turning their feelings around and giving themselves a *psychological recharge.*

I thought it would be interesting to find out exactly what 'quick-fix' strategies such people routinely use. Initially I thought I might approach some famous high achievers and ask them for their secrets. On second thoughts I decided it would be much more interesting and probably more useful to gather some tips from a very wide range of people with whom I am acquainted both in Great Britain and in Spain. I therefore chose to ask people whom I consider to have a high degree of self-motivation because they have *achieved so much often against very difficult odds.*

All the people whom I have included in this chapter have had many of life's cards stacked against them. Their problems have been as various as their backgrounds, lifestyles and their successes. Some have battled with personal difficulties such as ill-health, childhood deprivation, divorce and disabled children. Others have succeeded in their chosen work in spite of 'dog-eat-dog' cultures, discrimination and almost no financial backing. Many of these people have not only managed to motivate themselves successfully but are also renowned for their skill at developing self-motivation in others.

I am sure you will notice, as indeed I did, that although there are some common themes such as relaxation and positive self-talk, there is great variety in the kind of quick-fixes used by this selection of people. I suppose I should not have been surprised by this result because, as you already know, one of the traits I most appreciate in self-motivated people is their individuality.

I found this whole research exercise very stimulating and can't wait to try out some of the suggested quick-fixes for myself. I would highly recommend that you *undertake a similar route for yourself*. You could add to this list of encouraging tips by asking successful people whom you know for their secrets. You may find that some of your friends will have to think quite hard about what they do. Their 'quick-fix' may have become a habit without their having given it any conscious thought. But isn't it true that what seems like ordinary 'common sense' to one person can prove a new life-line to others?!

The question which I asked each individual was:

After a setback or low-period, what is your favourite trick for giving yourself a psychological boost and reviving your motivation?

As I knew that this book was likely to be read by people from a wide variety of cultures, I asked them to exclude religious practices.

You will notice that, finally, I decided to turn my question inwards, so the last 'Quick-fix' is my own. Although my strategies have served me well for many years, doing this research helped me see that I am ready to try some fresh ideas. Hopefully this collection will also help you to reflect on the effectiveness of your own strategies and perhaps stimulate some new thoughts for you as well.

Quick-fix Strategies Used by Successful Self-motivators

Cheryl Buggy, Radio Presenter

- I use a set of personal affirmations to turn any black negative moods around.
- I keep a 'scrapbook' which I consider to be a celebration of the best of me. It contains specially chosen photos, quotations, pictures and poems which help me instantly recall past achievements; people whom I love and places which I love to visit. When I am low I dip into this.
- I make contact with a good buddy.

Brian Baldwin, International Marketing Director for a telecommunications company

- I remind myself that it is important not to dwell on negative aspects of situations and that it is better to put them behind me and move on.
- I immediately look to see if there is anything positive which I can salvage from the situation.
- I immerse myself in the next project which comes up and am always amazed at how the new challenge makes me motivated all over again.
- I remind myself that the most important thing is to believe in yourself and that the harder I work the luckier I become.

Eileen Campbell, Publisher and Writer

- First of all I remind myself of everything I have achieved to date and tell myself how fortunate I am.
- Then I tell myself that there is nothing wrong with setbacks – they are opportunities to try again and that life is about learning and that *everything* is grist for the mill.

Tracey Sheppard, Freelance Glass Engraver

- I do something totally practical and usually active. A physical activity but one which is not distracting, such as a thorough house-clean or gardening.
- I renew my sense of security by welcoming friends and family to my home.

Dennis Elkins, Owner/Manager of his own 'odd-job' family business

- I sit down and relax and unwind.
- I focus on trying to clear my head by letting my mind go blank. I often play some classical music to help me do this.
- I then tell myself that if I keep my determination and self-respect, I will succeed in my business and my life.

Jan Hildebrand, Director of her own design consultancy

- For years I have kept a diary where I write out my feelings and attach inspirational clippings. I 'boost' myself by reading these passages – particularly when I have 'made it through'.
- I then write out my current feelings, putting them into perspective, and make an action plan for moving forward.

Ann Hauser, Architect with her own practice

- Minor or small setbacks are often dealt with by a good 'deck-clearing' project, either in the office or at home (emptying in-trays, tidying my desk or clearing cupboards).
- For larger setbacks I discuss the problem with friends in the same business to help me gain a wider view of the problem.
- When I am low in motivation, I know it is very important to get lots of sleep.

John Simpson, Ship's Master for large ferry company (and my kid brother!)

- I distract myself by getting totally immersed in an urgent project at work or at home. Doing this helps restore my self-confidence and lifts some of the gloom.
- I 'escape' for a period into a book, play or music and then make a decision to either fix [the problem] or live with it.

Helen Horton, Director of a Council for Community Service

- I speak to myself fiercely. I've tried a number of phrases and quotations, but the one which works best is: 'Rise above it!'
- I find a change in the rhythm can prevent the downward slide. When I am very tired and my energy levels are low, I have a snack and then deliberately go and do something active for an hour such as riding my bike or digging the allotment.

Jessica Stockham, Illustrator and Manager of her own business

- I try to appreciate the setback in a positive way by seeing it as a building block in the learning curve destined for something better.
- I then apply this new wisdom as appropriately as possible while keeping busy so that I don't lose momentum.

Peter Trebett, Warehouse Manager and Open University student

- To keep my motivation moving, I have to look at my goal and link it to another goal beyond what I am striving for now.
- When my motivation 'stalls', I always take a period of 'time out' to rebuild my energy again. This may be just ten minutes for a cup of tea or it could be a whole day away.

Avril Faulkner, retired teacher and Chairwoman of a charity

- First (in solitude!) I indulge myself in beating the hell out of a cushion or kicking my legs while screaming!
- Secondly, I treat myself to something 'sinful'.
- Thirdly, I sit down quietly with paper and pen and try to visualize how I would like things to be different and ask myself what step I can take today towards achieving my final goal.

Sue Johansson, Chartered Secretary for a utilities company

- I give myself a free day and indulge in one of my favourite hobbies.
- I allow myself some time for 'new ideas dreaming'.
- I ensure that the next activity which I carry out is something that I know I can do well – be it social, domestic or at work – then I let the quality of the result speak for itself!

- I take another look at my Life Plan (set out in its own special folder) to see if it has been affected, and then start my next Life Plan project. I remind myself of my motto 'Work at the future, now' as I believe that forward life-planning does reduce some of the uncertainties.
- I make sure that I am using positive and not negative language. I avoid using words like 'setback', 'flagging' and disappointment' and instead talk about 'varying levels of success/strength/results/happiness', etc.

Juan Sosa Gutiérrez, Owner/Manager of his own builder's merchant business

- My secret for overcoming difficulties and stopping myself from making them seem worse than they are, is to start thinking of how to deal with them better next time.
- If the situation is irreparable, I help myself accept it by saying 'that's life' and comfort myself with thoughts of my close-knit family. I often also recall the memories I have of my childhood, which are good in spite of the fact that things were not easy and you had to work very hard to get anything at all.

Isabel Melo, mother of four successful children and Church Counsellor

- I renew my strength by thinking of the love I have for my husband.
- I think about my children and their life-plans.
- I take a stroll into the country.
- I read something relaxing which will take my mind off the problem.
- I think of my parents and the way of life they used to have.
- I listen to good music.
- I remind myself that life will go on in spite of what has happened and that it doesn't help to dwell on negative things.

Miguel Hernández, Entrepreneur and Owner/Manager of a restaurant

- I look again at the idea behind what I am doing. I ask myself if it is really feasible to go on. If it is, I make a list of priorities and then get organized.
- I am also helped by looking back at my past and appreciating my successes and seeing what I have learned from them.

Malcolm VandenBurg, Physician and CEO of a clinical research company

- When my motivation is low, my usual strategy is to see if I can delegate that task and find a new one for myself.
- If delegation is not possible, I first take action to get relaxed and then make sure I reward myself at each milestone throughout the task.
- When the task is completed I have a bonus reward which usually involves having some fun.

Ari Badaines, Psychotherapist and Trainer, leading own international consultancy

- I remind myself that I am ultimately responsible for my choices.
- I ask how important this is to me. If it is not, I decide to drop it.
- I look at how I am stopping myself from achieving what I want.
- I remind myself that the process of working for my goal may be more important (as well as fun and informative) than the outcome.
- I visualize myself succeeding.
- When I am not successful, I encourage myself to accept it and remind myself that I am still the same person.

John Winterburn, Chartered Engineer for a telecommunications company

- I remind myself that experience has taught me that 'low-periods' and 'setbacks' are generally short-lived and that new challenges follow on quickly.
- During any low period it is important for me to keep in regular contact with my 'support group' (my friends, family and trusted colleagues). I find that their motivation carries me along for a while.

Nick Hodges, Operations Director of a finance company

- I find walking in the fresh air is very 'soul cleansing' and provides me with uninterrupted thinking time. If a big fix is required, I head for the Yorkshire Dales; if a little one will do, I walk around the city.
- Alternatively I use music as a solace – especially Bach.

Stuart Louden, Personnel Officer for a County Council

I use my own mnemonic to help reaffirm my self-respect:

Say positive things to myself and others.
Enjoy my family.
Live life to the full.
Forget my troubles and just be happy.

Remember the worse off.
Esteem build – in myself and others.
Succeed in something (anything will do for starters).
Practise relaxation.
Eliminate negative thought.
Contact friends.
Try something different.

Liz Wilson, Director of a university business school

- I reflect on the fact that many people would love to have my job and my problems, and that I have a great deal to be thankful for.
- I take time to consider my job in a wider context. When I place the problem in the context of a larger time horizon, low points immediately seem really rather insignificant.
- After a low period, I go into the country and converse with nature.

Gael Lindenfield, Writer, Psychotherapist and Training Consultant

- I 'lie low' for a while and give myself some time to wallow in my feelings while taking comfort from some simple everyday pleasures such as having a hot bubbly bath with a good book.
- I listen to some music which is *in tune* with my mood and my needs (releases my tears/soothes away tension/blasts out my frustration or uplifts my spirit).
- I 'waste' away an evening (sometimes a whole weekend!) curled up on the sofa watching TV soaps, chat-shows or a video with my family.
- I activate myself by doing something practical and very useful but undemanding, and quite unrelated to the problem (cleaning the kitchen, dead-heading flowers, catching up on non-urgent letters).
- I look at my diary and start reorganizing my life, as I know that nowadays most of my motivation setbacks are simply due to overload.

Instant Exercise: Quick-fixes

1 Note down your own favourite quick-fixes.
2 Select one or more new ideas from those listed above which you would like to try out.
3 Have a go next time you need recharging!

3

How to Encourage
Self-motivation in Others

Each of us has the capacity to be a leader. Many of us already lead a family, group or team of some sort, and we can of course be leaders through our ideas and influence, beside being a boss in a formal hierarchy.

DR HARRY ADLER

Introduction

Many of you reading this book will be concerned not just with your own levels of self-motivation, but also with making sure that other people in your life are successful self-motivators as well. Your livelihood, self-esteem or happiness could depend on other people's performance. Perhaps you are, for example:

- a *manager* at work and your very livelihood depends on your staff's achievements
- a *teacher* whose performance is continually being judged on your pupil's ability to push themselves into achieving certain academic results
- a *captain or coach* of a sports team and you cannot achieve the level of competence you want unless others are as committed as you are to maintaining high standards
- a *leader* of a political or community action group and you cannot effect the changes you desire without others maintaining the same level of dedication to the cause as yourself
- a *parent* and your happiness feels very dependent on your children's ability to thrive and reach their potential

As most of these roles fall into one of two broad categories – *leadership or parenting*, I have used these as my focus in the two parts of this section. But as you read I hope you will also be thinking of ways in which you can apply some of the ideas to other areas of your life. Even if we do not have a formal responsibility to encourage and boost the self-motivation of *friends, colleagues and neighbours*, it is often something we would like to be able to do simply because we care about them and *want* them to be successful and happy.

Self-motivational Leadership: A Dozen Guidelines

Motivation can never be forced. People have to want to do a good job.

DALE CARNEGIE

The following guidelines and tips have been drawn from a variety of sources. First I have incorporated some ideas from other writers and research in the field of motivation. Secondly I have used ideas arising directly as a result of my own personal trial-and-error experience as a leader.

My third source has been drawn more indirectly. It is an accumulated mass of moans and groans from demotivated people! You can imagine what an interesting challenge it is to translate these negative experiences into some positive advice!

In my confidential listening roles as both therapist and trainer, I hear the truth of what happens behind the closed doors of very many different organizations. I know that, often in spite of good intentions, many of the current everyday practices of leaders are counter-productive to self-motivation. So although some of the tips may seem obvious, every single one I have written has been inspired by repeated 'real-life' experiences of demotivating leadership practice.

I have listed below a dozen guidelines and suggested *some* ways in which these can be translated into action. As you are reading, try yourself to think of other practical ways in which these general guidelines can be integrated into various other leadership roles.

1. Define a Common Sense of Purpose

❏ Regularly discuss long-term goals to keep everyone's vision of success firmly implanted in their minds. While acknowledging some individual differences, select and reaffirm the shared aspects of everyone's purpose (such as, 'Although we all have our different reasons for wanting to work/study/play here, it seems that one [or more] aim we all share is…and the values we have in common are…').

❏ In consultation with a small, genuinely representative working party, translate and summarize the above into a short, easily understood 'mission statement' (see the books in Section 4 to gather ideas, or consult experts on the subject).

❏ Display your mission statement prominently and draw regular attention to it (on brochures, headed paper, large posters, pens, T shirts, mugs, etc.).

❏ Discuss and review your vision regularly with your team. In our fast-changing world it makes sense to check and perhaps adapt our long-term goals on an annual or bi-annual basis. This is especially true if the membership of your team or group is changing, or if the people in it are developing at a fast pace.

❏ Continually relate current objectives to long-term goals and/or more interesting tasks, especially when these may seem tedious or irrelevant ('Although, doing XYZ is not a job anyone of us *wants* to do, doing it quickly and efficiently will help us in the long run because…').

2. Create an Inspiring Environment

❏ Make sure that the team or group is consulted about any new plans for their environment (such as a new colour scheme). An office, headquarters or meeting room which feels 'alienating' will dampen self-motivation and initiative.

❏ Make sure that your environment reflects your *shared* sense of purpose and values (for example, if 'mutual support' is one of your values, check that the layout of seating and desks encourages this; if super-efficiency is of prime importance, check that your environment makes this easy for your team or group to implement; if refurnishing a rest area, make sure that comfort and tranquility are not sacrificed in favour of bargains or fashionable colour schemes).

❏ Regularly check out that the environment is meeting the needs of the group and ask for suggestions if it isn't. Never impose changes without consultation or a reasonable explanation as to why they have to be made.

3. Set Achievable Challenges

❏ Give as much responsibility as is realistically possible to the group for maintaining and caring for their own and shared space.

❏ Encourage the use of the following SMART mnemonic guide for team goal-setting. You could give each person a copy of the following:

SMART: Guidelines for Group Goals

When helping your group to set their goals together, check that they are:

S tretching

Self-motivation is greatest when we sense that our goals are enhancing our potential. Try to get the group to set goals which will ensure that everyone is stretched. But as very few teams are lucky enough to be made up of individuals who have equal potential or are at the same point in their development, there must be some room for flexibility. As the leader you should help each individual monitor his or her 'challenge' and 'boredom' thresholds, and then adapt the team's shared goals accordingly (that is, give high achievers more responsibility, those who are struggling slightly less).

M easurable

When setting goals, encourage people to think about *how* they can best assess their own progress. Point out when they are setting themselves goals which are too general and not easy to measure (for example, a goal such as 'This term/month let's all try to improve our communication' could become: 'This month let's try keeping a duplicate copy of all messages and each of us take responsibility for double-checking that our messages have been received. This will give us a clearer idea of where and when problems occur, and at the next meeting we can bring our duplicate copies and…').

As a leader you can also encourage your team to measure their progress by giving your regular reports in specific language (for example, instead of 'You're doing really well' you might say 'We are 75 per cent along the road. Did you think we had got that far?').

A ccepted

The team will be much more self-motivated if they have the reasoning behind their aims and targets explained, and have a chance to question and jointly approve them. (Obviously this is an ideal, and consensus goal-setting is not *always* practical.)

R ecorded

Research has proved that written goals are much more likely to be achieved, so as leader you should ensure that all goals are clearly and concisely recorded. They should then be displayed somewhere *everyone* in the group can and will read them (minutes of decision-making meetings can be put up on communal notice-boards, or sent out as an E-mail or paged message, instead of being filed away and forgotten until the next meeting).

[T] imed

We all know that goals are much more inspiring if there is a challenging deadline attached to them. But autocratically imposed deadlines do not encourage self-motivation, so the time-frame should, ideally, be set in consultation with the individuals in the team or group whenever possible.

4. Encourage Self-reliance

❑ Use language which shows that you assume people have the ability to achieve (for example, 'Although this is a new challenge for you, I am convinced that you will be able to meet it' – *not* 'I don't know if this is going to be too demanding for you').

❑ Provide or recommend training courses, books and cassettes which will teach self-help methods for boosting confidence.

❑ Give honest feedback when you see people damaging their own confidence (self-put-downs, negative talk, not doing adequate preparation, etc.).

❑ Make it easy for people to share their feelings when they lack self-confidence, but don't immediately assume that it's your job to build it up for them. While always emphasizing that each person has to be responsible for his or her own feelings, you can express your willingness to give *requested* support and help.

❑ Share your own past and current confidence-boosting secrets.

5. Value Individual Contribution

❑ Take the trouble to get to know by what name people like to be called, and encourage the frequent use of these names (as when making a request or giving feedback).

❏ Refer to and ask people to reflect on their individual strengths and potential contribution.

❏ Reinforce people's commitment to using their individuality by adapting job titles and job descriptions to reflect the above whenever possible.

❏ When interviewing and appraising, ask team members if there is any special aspect of the job which *they* think that they do well, or could do well. Ask the same questions concerning their weak areas.

❏ Keep training programmes as flexible as possible to allow individuals to develop at their own pace in their areas of most need. Choose trainers and coaches who are willing and able to adapt their programmes to suit each group and make allowances for each individual's specific needs and approach. (Beware of trainers selling 'fool-proof' blue-printed strategies more suitable for programming robots than encouraging individual initiative!)

6. Foster Group Belonging

❏ Use 'we' rather than 'I' language whenever you can and encourage others to do similarly.

❏ Have regular meetings – but keep them lively, task-orientated and as short as possible!

❏ Share your own positive experiences of working in a team and give specific examples of how, in the past, collaboration has grown out of individual ideas and effort.

❏ Consult before organizing social events to ensure maximum attendance, involvement and enjoyment.

7. Keep Communication Flowing

❏ Share your own news regularly and do 'spot-checks' to ensure that it is actually being heard by everyone.

❏ Make sure memos/letters, newsletters, etc. are easy and interesting to read. With desk-top publishing now so

cheap and easy, there is no longer an excuse for even
the simplest of written communication to appear wordy
and boring.

❑ Give rewards (if only praise and admiration) for
individual people who communicate well or have
ideas about how to improve communication.

❑ When being critical of poor communication, ensure that
you are also constructive and give suggestions on how
improvements could be made.

❑ Encourage development of skills, suggesting or
subsidizing courses in or books on, for example, listening,
letter writing and presentation.

❑ When giving information or instructions yourself, lead by
example – communicating effectively and offering clear
explanations as often as you can.

8. Give Meaningful Feedback

❑ Always be open and direct.

❑ Make the feedback frequent and as near to 'the event' as
possible (that is, don't wait for the September appraisal
session to commend August's good performance, and
don't hang around waiting for 'an opportune moment'
to give your criticism).

❑ Choose a setting and timing when your feedback will
be given the serious attention it deserves (resist the
temptation to slip in a compliment or criticism to a casual
social conversation).

❑ Use assertive strategies to fend off requests for feedback
at the 'wrong time' or in the wrong place (in too casual
a setting, for example, or when you are too distracted by
more pressing agendas).

❑ Set a positive tone to feedback by outlining at the outset
the possible benefits not just for you and the team or
organization, but for the individual, if high-quality
performance is maintained or achieved.

❑ Encourage self-appraisal as much as possible, but do not use it to shirk your responsibility for giving honest, direct feedback as well.

9. Stimulate and Reward Creativity

❑ Welcome *all* new ideas and suggestions and explain that, even if they are not used, they could stimulate the birth of ones which can be used.
❑ Encourage *everyone* to make time for periods of creative thinking.
❑ Make having fun at work routine (if not compulsory!). Explain your reasons for doing so to the workaholics and cynics so they do not sabotage themselves or others.

10. Give Generous and Fair Rewards

❑ Try to keep everyone's reward schemes flexible enough so that they can be in line with achievements (that is, don't reward only the front-line salesforce, directors or 'glamorous' key players).
❑ Make allowances for difficult periods your team has been through. Flexible bonus schemes should take into account the fluctuating demands of the marketplace.
❑ Consult team members or representatives whenever it is practical on even minor adjustments to reward schemes (or at the very least, give reasonable explanations for these adjustments).
❑ Do not allow reward schemes to become ridiculously top-heavy (such as ones where the most senior people take the lion's share of any profit or incentive scheme).
❑ Ensure that everyone has an equal opportunity to participate in incentive schemes and fun motivational events, and that if they choose not to be involved, they are given some compensation (people who do not see a day's

go-kart racing or a seat at the opera or tennis championships as a reward could and should be offered an alternative!).

11. Make Recuperation and Renewal Easy

❏ Set aside quiet rest areas to which *everyone* has access.
❏ Talk about lunch and other breaks as though you expect them to be regularly taken (for example, 'No, I can't see you until 2.30, because I am just off to lunch' / 'I'd like to talk something over quite urgently, but I don't want to intrude on your break so could we schedule it for...?').
❏ Provide accessible and inviting kitchenettes and dining areas where individuals can prepare snacks to their *own* taste if they choose to do so.
❏ Subsidize health club memberships.
❏ Give holidays as rewards and incentives.
❏ Reinforce the value of relaxing 'switch-off' periods by talking about how refreshing and energizing your holidays and weekends have been and then asking your team members if theirs have been equally so.

12. Be an Inspiring Role-model

❏ Take time to use the list of 36 Personality Drivers to review regularly your own self-motivation and behaviour.
❏ Don't pretend to be a faultless model. Be honest and genuine about your own dips in self-motivation, *but* always add what you are doing to rectify the situation.
❏ Ask your team to help with your own problems and bad habits regarding motivation ('Can you tell me when you hear me putting myself down or you think I am over- or under-working?').

Instant Exercise:
Self-motivational Leadership

- Having read and studied the above guidelines, formulate three step-by-step goals for yourself (keep them SMART!).
- Share these goals with a colleague (or your team) and ask for help and support in putting them into action and assessing your progress.

You don't claim leadership, you earn it!

SHEILA MURRAY BETHEL

Self-motivational Parenting

The idea that we, as parents or teachers, are programmers of our children's minds isn't idle speculation – it is scientific fact...of all the influences that predict your child's future, the most important influence is you.

SHAD HELMSTETTER

Although I have very little direct professional experience of working with children, I have worked with the 'inner child' of many hundreds of despairing demotivated adults. So in writing this chapter I have drawn on the wisdom I have gained through these experiences as well as 'hands-on' knowledge I have gained through being a parent myself.

When an adult's motivation consistently seems to need someone else to 'love' or 'kick' it into action, I have always found the seeds of the problem can be traced back to childhood. A child whose achievements have only ever been valued in relation to their power to please or placate parents, teachers, etc. will become an adult whose motivation is rarely experienced as an inner drive which can be controlled autonomously. This person will have certain beliefs about motivation embedded in his or her subconscious:

'There's no point in trying anything unless you can be sure that others will reward you fairly and/or handsomely.'

'The only good reason for making an effort to act responsibly is to minimize the risk of being punished or hurt by others.'

It wasn't until I had children myself that I realized how easy it is to become the kind of parent who sets such beliefs in her children's subconscious!

In spite of my knowledge of child psychology, when I was

first a parent I regularly succumbed to the temptation of motivational 'carrots and sticks'. The more important the goal (mine or theirs), the more tempting it was to use them. It was *relatively* easy to use the 'correct' self-motivational parenting behaviour to deal with messy bedrooms and issues over personal appearance. But when I started to get anxious about academic progress or physical self-care, I found myself resorting to promise upon promise and threat after threat.

These personal experiences helped me to appreciate that rarely are the mistakes parents make with regard to motivating their children malicious in any way. They are often made because they care deeply about their children and want to ensure that they have the very best survival skills. Many parents do not even realize the harmful long-term effects on *self*-motivation of relying too heavily on the carrot-and-stick strategies. Many more know and appreciate the value of encouraging self-motivation, but are so over-stressed or fearful themselves that they find it hard to resist the short-term benefits of the more crude approaches.

I am therefore aware that the exercise in this chapter could help some of you develop a few *new* useful strategies and behaviours. The rest of you, I hope, will welcome the opportunity to review and assess how well you put your good parenting intentions into practice!

Getting Started

Assuming that you have, for some time, been experiencing difficulty in getting your child to complete a specific task or to become more generally self-motivated, these are the steps I would first advise you to take.

Step 1

Immediately stop telling your children what *they* should or not do. Throwing words at 'deaf ears' will always make the problem worse, not better.

Step 2

Turn your concern inwards and consider what changes or positive action *you* can take.

Step 3

Take your focus off the current specific problem and take a more general look at your child's life and progress. This kind of review often tackles the problem more effectively in the long term, because it reveals root causes.

I know just how hard it is to take these kinds of steps when you are already emotionally and physically worn out. I have therefore devised a tool, in the form of a checklist, which I hope will make it easier to get started.

Parenting Partners

Obviously it would be useful to do the following exercise together with your co-parent. If this is not possible, a supportive and like-minded friend who is also concerned to improve his or her child's motivation is just as good.

Alternatively, this could be an excellent 'homework' exercise to do in a group, say at your local Parent and Toddler group, Parents' Association, baby-sitting circle, etc.

Preparation

Read the following checklist several times and then give yourself approximately one week's thinking and self-observation time before completing it. Limit your reflection to a specific period of time (perhaps the events of the past month or week).

The Checklist Questions

You will note that under each heading I have given some examples of questions you could use to check your functioning in this area. But please remember that it is important that this self-assessment is relevant to you and your children. You could formulate some additional appropriate questions of your own. Re-reading the list of self-motivating Drivers could be a useful prompt.

Scoring

Assess the adequacy of your parenting behaviour in each area by putting ticks and crosses in the boxes. Alternatively, you could rate yourself on a numbered scale or percentages. The latter method might help you to monitor yourself more accurately.

The 3 × 3 'T' Test

I have selected three areas of parenting which I believe are most relevant to self-motivation. Each section has three key words to use as a focus for your self-questioning. As each word begins with 'T' (for 'Test'!), I hope you will find them easy to commit to memory.

1: Trust, Tolerance and Truth
– The Nurturing Relationship

Through my relationship with my children, am I providing enough:

❑ **TRUST?**
 – Am I giving them enough scope and encouragement to do things on their own?
 – How often do I assure them verbally of my confidence in their abilities and their potential?
 – Do I let them know that I trust that they can find their own levels of strength and weakness?
❑ **TOLERANCE?**
 – Am I communicating a clear message that it is OK for

my children to make and learn from their own mistakes?

– Am I making it clear that they are different from me and I enjoy their individuality?
– Am I giving them the opportunity to consider and test out values and ideas with which I do not myself agree?
– Am I allowing them to stick long enough in the states of muddle and confusion so that they have a real chance of producing their own creative ideas?

❑ **TRUTH?**
– Am I giving them honest feedback or do I sometimes tread too softly for fear of hurting their feelings or disturbing the peace?
– Am I giving too rosy, or too warped, a view of the world and the people in it?
– Do I make some tasks seem harder or easier than they really are?

2: Temptation, Thrills and Treats
– The Inspiring Environment

Am I providing enough:

❑ **TEMPTATION?**
– Are there enough books, magazines, pictures, videos, tapes, CDs, etc. around at home which might kindle their interest?
– Am I giving them exposure to the long-term benefits of working, practising, etc.? Could I give them a real-life taste of the fruits of the kind of success they are seeking?
– Am I giving them an opportunity to meet with relevant inspiring achievers?

❑ **THRILLS?**
– Am I ensuring that everyday life is as exciting as it can be?
– Am I making sure that they have enough easy short-term goals so that they regularly feel the 'buzz' that accompanies achievement?
– Could I do something to help them make boring homework assignments or repetitive revision more

stimulating and fun?

– Is the balance of our holiday time together too heavily weighted towards recovery for me? Is there adequate time left for having shared exciting, challenging experiences?
– Are there enough opportunities to taste the thrill of discovery and adventure?

❏ **TREATS?**

– Are they getting enough or too many treats?
– Are the treats I arrange still appropriate for their age and current interests? Have I been so busy or involved in the 'treat' myself that I haven't taken the time to check this out with my children?
– Am I ensuring that treats are not always bought with money and that my children are learning that sometimes the best treats cost nothing?
– Am I making sure that the treats are not always just given as rewards for success? Do I make sure that there are also treats during the toughest periods when they are most needed?
– Am I encouraging my children to treat themselves or am I holding on too tightly to my power in this respect?
– Am I always careful to make sure that there is adequate time-out for emotionally healing treats after a setback or disappointment, or do we tend to rush too quickly into the next challenge?

3: *Tools, Tactics and Tests: Practical Training*

Am I ensuring that my children are being provided with adequate:

❏ **TOOLS?**

– Do my children have adequate up-to-date aids which will help them complete their work?
– Have I any unfair expectations because I managed or other children managed to achieve success without extra books/a computer/a cricket bat, etc.?

❏ **TACTICS?**

    – Am I spending enough time with my children helping them plan out tactics to solve problems, handle relationship difficulties, or manage their emotions?

    – Do I rush in too quickly with my ideas of what ought to be done?

    – Am I too tempted to rush in with 'band-aid' solutions when I feel the pain of my children's distress?

    – Do I watch to make sure that my children are using step-by-step approaches?

❏ **TESTS?**

    – Am I making sure that my children are monitoring their progress?

    – Am I careful not to rush in with my own judgements before they have had time to appraise their own progress?

    – Am I giving them plenty of practical opportunities to try out their skills and ideas in relatively safe situations so that they can avoid unnecessary, embarrassing failures?

    – Am I ensuring that my children have a chance to have their performance assessed by objective people who are also skilled in the subject they are pursuing?

    – Do I know for sure that their teachers and coaches are competent and willing to give them useful objective assessments?

    – Do I make it clear to my children that not all tests, competitions or assessments are fairly judged? Do I make sure that I take the time to show them how to deal with and recover from unfair testing?

Instant Exercise:
Self-motivational Parenting

• Review all your scores in each of the three areas, and then make a list of the areas which need some attention.

• Write down three specific realistic goals for yourself. Choose according to priority and/or achievability. (Don't try and change either your own or your children's entire life at once!)

- Share these with someone, and ask for help in monitoring your progress. If you have a parenting partner he or she may be the best choice, though equally this may not be the case if you have different ideas on the subject of motivation.
- Write the three sets of key words on a card and memorize them to help you stay on the right self-motivational track!

To be a good enough parent one must be able to feel secure in one's parenthood, and in relation to one's child. So secure that while one is careful in what one does in relation to one's child, one is not over-anxious about it and does not feel guilty about being a good-enough parent.

BRUNO BETTLEHEIM

4

Further Help

*Other resources which would aid and
support the development of self-motivation*

Books

Dr Harry Adler, *Think Like a Leader* (Piatkus, 1995)

Dr Robert Anthony, *Doing What You Love, Loving What You Do* (Berkley Books, 1991)

D. A. Benton, *Lions Don't Need To Roar* (Warner Books, 1992)

Sheila Murray Bethel, *Making a Difference – 12 Qualities that Make You a Leader* (Berkley Books, 1990)

Bruno Bettleheim, *A Good Enough Parent* (Pan, 1987)

Jack Black, *Mindstore – The Ultimate Mental Fitness Programme* (Thorsons, 1994)

Tony Buzan, *Make the Most of Your Mind* (Pan, 1988)

Eileen Campbell, *A Dancing Star: Inspirations to Guide and Heal* (Thorsons, 1992)

—, *A Fabulous Gift:* (Thorsons, 1994)

—, *Healing Our Hearts and Lives* (Thorsons, 1995)

Allen Carmichael, *Believe You Can* (Concept, 1991)

Dale Carnegie, *The Leader in You* (Pocket Books, 1993)

Petruska Clarkson, *The Achilles Syndrome – Overcoming the Secret Fear of Failure* (Element Books, 1994)

Stephen R. Covey, *The 7 Habits of Highly Effective People* (Simon and Schuster, 1989)

Philippa Davies, *Personal Power* (Piatkus, 1991)

Roger Dawson, *The Confident Decision Maker* (Nightingale-Conant/William Morrow, 1993)

Richard Denny, *Motivate to Win* (Kogan Page, 1993)

Timothy R. V. Foster, *101 Great Mission Statements* (Kogan Page, 1993)

Dina Glouberman, *Life Choices and Life Changes Through Imagework* (Unwin Paperbacks, 1993)

Dr Kenneth Hambly, *Banish Anxiety* (Thorsons, 1991)

Shad Helmstetter, *Predicative Parenting, What to say When You Talk To Your KIds* (Pocket Books, 1989)

Napoleon Hill & W. Clement Stone, *Success Through A Positive Mental Attitude* (Thorsons, 1991)

Robert Holden, *Stress Busters* (Thorsons, 1992)

—, *Laughter, the Best Medicine* (Thorsons, 1994)

—, *Living Wonderfully* (Thorsons, 1994)

Barbara Jacques, *The Complete Colour, Style & Image Book*
  (Thorsons, 1994)
Susan Jeffers, *Feel The Fear And Do It Anyway*
  (Arrow Books, 1987)
Andrew Leigh and Michael Maynard, *Leading Your Team –*
  How to Involve and Inspire Others (Nicholas Brealey, 1995)
Gael Lindenfield, *Assert Yourself* (Thorsons, 1986)
—, *Super Confidence* (Thorsons, 1989)
—, *The Positive Woman* (Thorsons, 1992)
—, *Managing Anger* (Thorsons, 1993)
—, *Confident Children* (Thorsons, 1994)
—, *Self-esteem* (Thorsons, 1995)
Alan Loy McGinnis, *Bringing Out The Best in People*
  (Augsburg, 1985)
David McNally, *Even Eagles Need A Push* (Thorsons, 1993)
Ursula Markham, *Managing Conflict* (Thorsons, 1996)
Joseph V. Quigley, *Vision – How Leaders Develop, Share it,*
  and Sustain it (McGraw-Hill, 1993)
Vera Peiffer, *Positive Thinking* (Element Books, 1989)
Louis Proto, *Take Charge of Your Life* (Thorsons, 1988)
Anthony Robbins, *Awaken The Giant Within*
  (Simon and Schuster, 1992)
John-Roger and Peter McWilliams, *You Can't Afford the Luxury*
  of a Negative Thought (Thorsons, 1990)
Dorothy Rowe, *The Successful Self* (Fontana/Collins, 1988)
Anthony Storr, *Solitude* (HarperCollins, 1989)
Theodore Zeldin, *An Intimate History of Humanity*
  (Minerva, 1996)

Cassettes

The following cassettes are designed to complement my books.
Each one is a psychological exercise programme which should
be done on a regular basis. They can be played while driving
the car, having a bath or doing the housework or gardening.
I plan to supplement the list very soon.

Gael Lindenfield, *The Anger Control Workout* (Thorsons)
—, *The Positive Power Workout* (Thorsons)
—, *The Super Confidence Workout* (Thorsons)

Games

These are a fun method of doing personal development work. They could be especially useful for leaders, teachers and self-help groups. Here are some examples:

> *Futurestories* – a fun board game for all ages where you talk about yourself, your hopes and dreams for the future and how you see your life developing.
>
> *The Ungame* – a best-selling non-competitive board question game for all ages which is designed to develop communication skills.
>
> *The Love Game* – a game to help people express their true selves and build self-esteem.

All the above, plus many other games, books and cassettes designed to help people develop better emotional health are stocked by:

Being Yourself
73 Liverpool Road
Deal
Kent CT14 7NN
England
Tel. 01304 381333
Fax 01304 381255

Courses

Please contact my publishers if you would like details of my personal development courses for individuals, groups and organizations, or my centre in Spain.

5

Notebook

Driver 1: Visionary Thinking – without Idle Dreaming

Driver 2: Unashamed Neediness – without Selfish Greediness

Driver 3: Eternal Optimism – without Denying Common Sense

Driver 4: Guru-worshipping – without Blind Following

Driver 5: Sound Self-esteem – without Ignorant Arrogance

Driver 6: Thirst for Challenge – without Scorning Easy Options

Driver 7: Addiction to Achievement – without Imprudent Impatience

Driver 8: Steadfast Principles – without Narrow Prejudice

Driver 9: Consistent Courage – without Thoughtless Gambling

Driver 10: Endless Energy – without Debilitating Burnout

Driver 11: **Prepared Proactivity – without Disregard for Opportunity**

Driver 12: **Solid Responsibility – without Rigid Perfectionism**

Driver 13: Calm Concentration – without Repressed Creativity

Driver 14: Systematic Organization – without Obtuse Obsessionality

Driver 15: Meticulous Planning – without Stubborn Inflexibility

Driver 16: Sharp Decisiveness – without Blindness to Consequence

Driver 17: Slick Self-presentation – without Enslavement to Fashion

Driver 18: Positive Problem-solving – without Immunity to Despair

Driver 19: **Reliable Intuition –
without Acting on Every Hunch**

Driver 20: **Searching Self-reflection –
without Frustrating Self-absorption**

Driver 21: Pride in Individuality – without Disregard for Human Commonality

Driver 22: Deep Emotionality – without Enslavement to Feelings

Driver 23: **Stringent Self-criticism –**
without Suffocating Self-abuse

Driver 24: **Intolerance of Excuses –**
without Deafness to their Message

Driver 25: Sincere Self-forgiveness – without Self-inflicted Punishment

Driver 26: Personal Power – without Disempowering Others

Driver 27: Assertive Directness – without Thoughtless Insensitivity

Driver 28: Skilled Self-protection – without Harmful Aggression

Driver 29: **Perpetually Learning – without Devaluing Own Wisdom**

Driver 30: **Seriously Focused – without Humourless Solemnity**

Driver 31: Sensibly Self-nurturing – without Spurning Support

Driver 32: Seeker of Solitude – without Reclusive Aloofness

Driver 33: **Revelling in Success –
without Fear of Failure**

Driver 34: **Scrupulously Self-healing –
without Dismissing Comfort**

Driver 35: Amply Self-rewarding – without Rejecting Recognition

Driver 36: Inwardly Driven – without Scorning Incentives

How to Encourage Self-motivation in Others

Personal Development Action Plan

Index

acceptance 90–91, 187, 196
achievement:
    addictive (driver 7) 33–5, 222
    blocks to 187
    rewarding 200
    and self-esteem 25–6
    and short-term goals 207
action 51, 94–5
activity, physical 183, 184, 189
addiction:
    and guru-worship 21
    to achievement (driver 7) 33–5, 222
adrenalin 82
advice 152, 153
affirmation 141–2, 171
affirmations 11, 15–16, 31, 69, 83, 161,
    182, 183, 188
age, as target time 12
aggression *see* self-protection
aloofness *see* solitude
amends, making 128, 129
analysis techniques 81, 91–2, 121
    see also self-reflection
anger 116, 140–142
anticipation, expectant 17
apathy xi, 109, 176
appropriateness 59
arrogance *see* self-esteem
art 100
assertive directness (driver 27) 136–9,
    232
assertive techniques 16, 35, 47, 120,
    156, 166, 172, 199
attention span 63
awareness 114, 118–19

Badaines, Ari 187
baggage, unwanted 31
balance 57, 109, 155, 156, 158
Baldwin, Brian 183
behaviour, and powerlessness 132
behavioural norms 56

behavioural training 50, 114
belief, force of 4, 55
    see also self-belief
big-thinkers, tuning into 6
blocking 19, 61, 166
brain:
    stimulating 96
    using right and left sides 61, 82, 92,
    98–9, 101
brainstorming 76–7, 83, 92–3, 95
breaks 47, 63, 72, 80, 92, 105, 201
breathing 43
'Broken Record' technique 157
budgeting 93
Buggy, Cheryl 182
burnout 48
    see also energy

Campbell, Eileen 183
carrot-and-stick strategies 204
cathartic release 115, 185
celebrations 160, 161–2, 164
challenges xiv-xv, 161
    achievable 195
    (driver 6) 28–32, 221
    and failure 26
chance, synchronizing with 31
changes:
    beneficial 19
    of circumstances 10
    energy demands of 48
    long-term 14
    on-going 20
    responsibility needs 54
    to life xv
    vs spruce-up 88
    see also proactivity
channelling 167, 168
    constructive 115
children:
    getting stimulus from 16, 149
    see also parenting

Index